Writings from The Oval Table

Kathy Brooks
David Rasmussen
Doreen Tadros
Karen Shaw
Robert Ramsay

Writings from The Oval Table

Anthology

Copyright © 2019 Robert L. Ramsay
ISBN: 978-1-79621-434-5

All rights reserved. No part of this publication may be reproduced, stored in a retrieval system, or transmitted in any form or by any means, electronic, mechanical, recording, or otherwise, without the prior written permission of the author.

This collection of writings from The Oval Table includes fiction, creative nonfiction, essays and poetry. In the fictional works the names, characters, events, and dialogue are the product of the author's imagination or are used fictitiously. Any resemblance to actual persons, living or dead, is entirely coincidental.

First Edition

Writings from The Oval Table

Anthology

Dedicated with thanks to
Kathy Brooks
who kick-started the Oval Table
in 2013

and remembering
Oval Table member,

Memorial plaque
on a bench
in Dunsmuir Gardens
Surrey, BC

Table of Contents

Table of Contents 6

Forward 8

Kathy Brooks 11
   Go Danny Boy, Go 12

David Rasmussen 19
   Lady of the Night 20
   Much Have I Travelled 23
   Just a Coffee 30
   Umberto 34
   The Pump 36
   Sidewalk Café 41
   Earth Day 44
   Life's Sweet Moments 49

Doreen Tadros 53
   The Old Testament For Dummies 54
   A Night of Wonder 57
   The Girl Who Climbed the Mighty Oak 60

Karen Shaw 65
   The Cowards 66
   The Scrip 72
   Sharon and the Ball of String 78
   The Flood 83

Robert Ramsay 89
   A Sloppy Time on the High Iron 90
   Stone Walls 98
   Tall Tails 106
   The Problem of Self-Stimulation 111

Anthology

A Group Writing Exercise 117
    The Mysterious Affair at The Corner Café 118
POETRY 123

Forward

In the spring of 2013 Kathy Brooks proposed forming a writing group made up of writers who wished to have their work critiqued. She offered her home in White Rock, British Columbia as the venue. The group would meet every second Friday and membership would be limited to six people. That way everyone would have the opportunity to read and receive constructive criticism.

The original members were Kathy Brooks, Robert Ramsay, David Rasmussen, Karen Shaw, Eileen Spencer and Doreen Tadros.

The authors met around Kathy's oval-shaped dining room table, thus the name, *The Oval Table*, a shameless throwback to *The Round Table* of authors who met during the 1920s at the Algonquin Hotel in New York City. Thanks to the constructive criticism, several writers' stories and poems have won prizes in local contests. Included in this anthology are some of the prize-winning pieces.

Seated around The Oval Table
L to R: Robert Ramsay, Doreen Tadros, Karen Shaw,
Eileen Spencer, Kathy Brooks, David Rasmussen

Writings from The Oval Table

Anthology

Kathy Brooks

Go Danny Boy, Go
Kathy Brooks

The three boys stretched out on the railroad tracks, ears pressed to the rails.

"Listen," Sam said. "If there's a train coming, the tracks will vibrate."

"Yeah, I saw Tonto do that on the *Lone Ranger*," Derek said.

"Nah, I don't think it was Tonto," said Danny. "It was some cowboy movie."

"Shhh," Sam said. "We won't hear anything if you guys don't shut up."

They lay silently, concentrating. Derek and Danny sat up after a few moments, but Sam stayed with his ear to the rails. Then he jumped up. "Okay, let's go," he said.

Danny was designated to go first. The tunnel in front of them looked like a gaping black mouth, the drips off the top from the recent rain reminded Danny of saliva.

"Hurry up, Danny," said Sam, giving him a push toward the tunnel.

They had watched trains come through the tunnel blasting their way out of the blackness, barely clearing the tunnel sides. If a train came while he was in there, Danny knew he'd be squished. The boys figured the tunnel was only a few hundred feet long. If it didn't curve, they would have been able to see the light at the far end, but it curved just enough that it was pitch black in the middle.

Danny took a deep breath, closed his eyes and walked forward. He held one arm out in front to ward off spider webs or any scaries that might jump out at him. He reached out the other arm and ran his hand along the tunnel wall as he walked. He wanted to run but he was afraid of falling on the uneven ground alongside the tracks. Sam had told him to walk on the ties, but Danny knew he wouldn't be able to touch the wall if he did that. Feeling the solid wall with his hand made him feel less alone in the tunnel.

His heart pounded in his chest. He stopped after ten steps, wanting to turn back. He swore he could hear a train coming. Behind him Sam and Derek were yelling, "Go Danny Boy, go!"

He plunged on, his nose filling with the moist air and the stale smell of diesel. His hand grazing the damp wall felt slime and crumbling dirt. The mucky ground seeped through his sneakers. The drip, drip of falling water echoed in the blackness.

He emerged out of the tunnel, one hand covered with soot, the light blinding him for a moment. He gulped the fresh air. He sank down on the grassy bank beside the tracks and waited for Sam and Derek.

A few moments later, the sun caught Sam's red hair as he emerged from the tunnel. Sam looked calm as if he was just out for a Sunday stroll. Soon after, Derek came scrambling out of the tunnel, his gangly legs flying. He ran for the grassy bank and collapsed beside Danny.

That summer, when they were twelve years old, they ran the tunnel a dozen times. Sam, being the tallest and looking older than his age, was the boss, and when he said they were going to the tunnel, Derek and Danny just nodded and followed him.

Many years later, Danny thought maybe Sam had craved a thrill, an escape from his boring life. His parents were both invalids after a car accident, and so Sam and his older sister had to cook, clean and do whatever parents usually did. Sam rarely had time for any fun.

Danny knew why he and Derek did it. They respected Sam and knew he had a tough life, and they wanted to please him. Sam was super-chatty after they ran the tunnel as if his system went into overdrive. The three of them would take a different route home through the woods, avoiding the tunnel, laughing, shouting and shoving each other. The black-mouthed tunnel would be forgotten for a few days.

Years later, Dan graduated from high school and moved two hundred kilometers away to go to college. His first day of classes, he hesitated outside the English 101 lecture hall. Through the open door he had caught a glimpse of a sloping row of chairs with small desks attached. There must have been over a hundred seats in there. He was tempted to turn around, but in his head, he heard the words, "*Go Danny Boy, go.*" He took a deep breath, closed his eyes for a moment and plunged in.

Dan's new life was absorbing and exciting. After a few futile attempts to keep in touch with Sam and Derek, he gave up. Before long, he realized that most people in his classes were new too, and he quickly made close friends.

Though he lived with his elderly Aunt Vivian, he managed to get out to the pub with his friends and get into a little trouble wandering home late at night, half-drunk. One time, they found some chalk and wrote rude words on the sidewalk outside Aunt V's house. The next morning, she huffed and puffed as she scrubbed the profanities off with a brush.

"I can't imagine the type of people who would do such a thing," she said. "Imagine the poor upbringing they must have had."

Dan pretended to sneeze to hide his smile.

His aunt nodded approvingly when she saw him writing or reading. He started to keep a notebook with him at all times to write down the new things he learned in biology or chemistry. He started doing it to avoid talking to Aunt Vivian, who was prone to lecturing rather than conversing. Soon, he looked forward to the times when he could write in his notebook; it helped him clarify the day's lessons. When it was time for exams, Dan realized he only needed to review his notes to get top marks.

Four years later, Dan graduated with a Bachelor of Science and started looking for work. He'd had a summer job in the geology labs at the university, but he wasn't confident that this experience would count for much. He persevered, filling out applications and working on his resumé. To his surprise he was asked to come for an interview with a local mining company. He spent many hours in the library, making up mock questions and answers, and studying books on interview skills, but nothing prepared him for what he confronted when he arrived at the company's office. When he walked down the hallway to take a seat, he caught a glimpse inside the interview room. To his shock, there wasn't one interviewer but five of them, seated behind a long table.

Waiting in the hallway outside the room, his heart thumped in his chest. He held a copy of his resumé between his shaking fingers. Because his hands were so sweaty, he was afraid the resumé would be ruined.

He was tempted to run, but when his name was called he heard the words echo in his head, *"Go Danny Boy, go."* He took a deep breath, closed his eyes for a moment, and plunged in.

Now in his late twenties, Dan was gaining seniority and feeling more confident in his job every day. He loved the travel out to the mine sites, the microscope work back in the office, the report writing. He was starting to save money and had managed to buy a car. He was sharing a spiffy apartment with a good friend.

The one thing he hadn't found was a soul mate. There had been a few girls along the way, but no one he felt crazy about. Was he too optimistic to think that the right girl would come along? Or was he being too choosy? He and his roommate discussed girls endlessly. Dan decided that the right girl would come along if he were patient. His roommate disagreed. "You gotta get out there, Dan, and be assertive—if you see a girl that attracts you, ask her out."

Dan was hoping that a girl would come to him so he wouldn't have to go fishing for one, but he didn't forget his roommate's advice. Maybe he needed to pay more attention.

Shopping for a take-out roast chicken one day after work, he looked up to see a girl about his age, examining the chickens. Dan thought her bright pink t-shirt contrasted nicely with her long, dark hair. She smiled at him as she grabbed a plump chicken right in front of him. He started to turn toward the checkout, then stopped. He took a deep breath, closed his eyes for a moment, and took the plunge.

"Hey, your chicken looks bigger than mine," he said.
Go Danny Boy, go!

Writings from The Oval Table

Anthology

David Rasmussen

Lady of the Night
David Rasmussen

The final chore of my day is taking out the garbage. We live on the first floor. It's a short walk down the hallway to the side exit of our apartment building. After tossing the bag of garbage into the large bin, I feel that my work has been done for the day.

I enjoy going out after dark. While standing outside in the quiet darkness, I take a moment to look up at the sky. If I'm fortunate enough to have a clear sky, I can see the occasional star. In some ways it is the most peaceful time of the day.

That is, until one evening this summer, when I walked, as usual, out the side exit of our building with a bag of garbage in hand. As I came around towards the front of the garbage shed, I heard a sound from inside. My first thought was that it was an animal—perhaps a dog, a raccoon, or possibly a rat. As I cautiously walked around to the front, I noticed that one of the two large doors to the shed was open.

The sound was much louder now. I could hear shuffling and scraping sounds. I cautiously peered into the shed. To my surprise, there was a frail, elderly woman. She wasn't very tall, and it was taking great effort for her to reach over the side of the large garbage bin. I realized that she had a long pole and was rummaging around the bags of garbage, unaware of my presence. It was then I noticed her walker was parked just inside the shed. I carefully tossed my bag into the bin, and quietly left.

Over the nights that followed, I often saw her poking through the garbage. I began excusing myself prior to throwing in my bag. I also began to notice some items placed on the 'seat' of her walker—a partial loaf of bread, an empty rum bottle, a jar of something…

I began saying, "Good evening" to her. She would pause momentarily to look at me. She looked as if she had led, and was still leading, a difficult life. After all, why would someone be rifling through garbage at night? Sometimes I encountered her going through the blue recycling bins, which, somehow, didn't seem to be as bad.

I knew she didn't live in our building. Or, perhaps it was just wishful thinking on my part that no one in our seniors' building would have to do this.

My wife and I talked about her. What could we do? Should we leave food out for her? Should we give her money?

Then, just the other evening, I went out on my garbage trip. I knew she was there, but this time she was at the front, just inside the shed. Her back was to me as she leaned into the bin, moving her pole around. For a moment I didn't know what to do. Should I toss the bag over her head?

No, I couldn't do that to this poor, starving woman. With bag in hand I turned around and headed back towards the side entrance. It was at that moment I ran into a friend, who was outside having a smoke. Initially, I hadn't seen him due to the darkness. He looked at me. He looked at my bag. I tried to explain that I just couldn't throw it over the woman's head. As he opened the door for me he was quietly laughing at the fact I was taking my garbage back inside.

As we walked down the hallway, he explained that the woman lives across our street at the seniors' special care facility, where she is well taken care of. He explained that she is a hoarder. She collects things and brings her highly-prized treasures back to her room. The care facility gets rid of them daily.

One part of me was relieved she wasn't starving. The other part of me felt sad, because she believes she has to dig through garbage every night.

Much Have I Travelled
David Rasmussen

> *Much have I travelled in the realms of gold,*
> *And many goodly states and kingdoms seen...*
> John Keats

It is the ninth day of July 2007. This morning I reached a golden milestone as I finished reading my fiftieth book—quite the journey for a brain injury survivor who, in the beginning, couldn't grasp the meaning of a sentence with more than a dozen words.

Although I lacked short-term memory, I had a strong desire to read. I remember when it all began…

I held the thin burgundy coloured book, *Memories of My Life in a Polish Village* by Toby Knobel Fluek. I leafed through the introductory pages until:

> *I was born and grew up on this farm in a rural village named Czernica in eastern Poland. My father's family had been there for generations.*

With the completion of this paragraph I began to struggle through my first book. At that time, I couldn't conceive that I would read fifty books over the next eight years. But I read one word at a time and the words became sentences and those sentences became paragraphs. The paragraphs became chapters, and chapters eventually became books.

As I continued to read, my ability to understand the words, the sentences and the paragraphs improved.

I have travelled word-by-word, page-by-page on this literary journey. And yes, many goodly states and kingdoms did I see. Beginning with Poland in 1930 I have journeyed…to the story of the world's oldest human footprints in the *Voices of Time* by Eduardo Galeano, the master of the vignette:

> *A couple was walking across the savannah in East Africa at the beginning of the rainy season. The woman and the man still looked a lot like apes, truth be told, although they were standing upright and had no tails.*

…with Julius Caesar in *Heroes of History* by renowned historian Will Durant:

> *…he summoned his favorite Thirteenth Legion…When he told them that he had no money with which to pay them, they emptied their savings into his treasury. On January*

> *10, 49 B.C., he led one legion across the Rubicon…*

✓

…to Geneva with the husband and wife writing team of Lawrence and Nancy Goldstone in *Out of the Flames:*

> *October 27, 1553, Michael Servetus was led to the stake… Servetus prayed silently… The fire was lit…*

…to 1607 on an English fleet bound for Sumatra and Java in search of spices in Nathaniel's *Nutmeg* by Giles Milton:

> *While the men on the Hector were busy mending ropes and caulking the decks, the crew of Keeling's vessel were learning speeches, sewing costumes and performing dress rehearsals. Finally, the big day arrived. Dropping anchor off the coast of Sierra Leone the dilettantish Keeling watched a final rehearsal and decided that his men were as good as they would ever be. A select audience was invited from the Hector and the play performed under the star-studded African sky. 'We gave,' wrote the proud captain, 'the tragedie of Hamlett.'…it must have been one of the earliest amateur performances of the play, staged not at the Globe Theatre but on the*

mangrove-tangled shores of equatorial Africa.

…to the high Canadian Arctic with John Rae, the Arctic adventurer who discovered the fate of Franklin, in *Fatal Passage* by Ken McGoogan:

The months passed rapidly. Far from the comforts and conviviality of civilization, Rae did his best to recreate the spirit of the Christmas season, choosing a meal of choice venison and deer's tongues with a small allowance of biscuit, plum pudding, and even a bit of brandy. The men worked up an appetite by playing football. On New Year's Day, 1854, they again amused themselves with football, though they left off sooner because a freak warm spell had briefly raised the temperature to eighteen degrees above zero Fahrenheit, which was far too warm for such antics.

…to Cairo in the early twentieth Century in *Echoes of an Autobiography* by Nobel Laureate, Naguib Mahfouz:

Death paid its first visit to our home when my grandmother died. Death was still something new: I had had no experience of it except in passing on the street.

Anthology

...in the trenches on the Western Front, Christmas Eve 1914, in *Silent Night* by Stanley Weintraub:

> *"It was a beautiful moonlit night, frost on the ground, white almost everywhere; and...there was a lot of commotion in the German trenches and then there were those lights— I don't know what they were. And then they sang 'Silent Night'— 'Stille Nacht'. I shall never forget it. It was one of the highlights of my life."*

...to 1953 with the momentous scientific paper by James D. Watson and Francis H. C. Crick, in the book *The Discoveries* by Alan Lightman:

> *We wish to propose a structure for the salt of deoxyribose nucleic acid (D.N.A.)...It has not escaped our notice that the specific pairing we have postulated immediately suggests a possible copying mechanism for the genetic material...*

...and finally to my birth place, Victoria, in the 1970's—and my fiftieth book—Alice Munro's, *The Love of a Good Woman*:

> *The rehearsals were held upstairs in an old building on Fisgard Street. Sunday afternoon was the only time that everybody could get there...While other people swam*

at Thetis Lake, or thronged Beacon Hill Park to walk under the trees and feed the ducks, or drove far out of town to the Pacific beaches, Jeffrey and his crew labored in the dusty high-ceilinged room on Fisgard Street.

Over these past eight years I have visited 'many goodly states and kingdoms'. And tomorrow I begin reading *The Mysterious Flame of Queen Loana*, a special gift, inscribed:

> *Happy Father's Day Dad*
> *Love Chris*
> *Umberto Eco's Final Novel*
> *The story of a man who,*
> *like you, seeks truth*
> *through literature.*

The back cover of the book reveals:

> *What if you woke up tomorrow and remembered nothing of your life? The faces of your spouse and children are strange, and the outlines of your childhood are only a blur. This is the crisis that Yambo, an Italian bookseller, faces when he regains consciousness after suffering a stroke.*

How appropriate—the story of a man dealing with a brain injury.

As I begin the journey towards my hundredth book, I wonder, what goodly states and kingdoms will I see?

Just a Coffee
David Rasmussen

She hurried along the sidewalk. *I wish I wasn't so nervous. What's wrong with me? After all this time I was just starting to get on with my life. And then, out of the blue, he calls.*

She entered the coffee shop. Inside it was quieter than usual. She saw him sitting at a table staring out the window. *Thank goodness, I'll have a moment to compose myself. Deep breathing.*

He turned and saw her. He stood up. They hugged as they always had, even although something seemed to be missing between them.

He looked at her and smiled. "Thanks for meeting me for coffee."

"No, thank you for inviting me, it's…it's wonderful to see you after all this—"

"I suppose it has been awhile. Please, sit down."

She sat down and then looked up at him and smiled.

He stood beside the table. "It's very nice to see you. What can I get you…your usual?"

"Yes, yes," she said. "You still remember?"

"Of course I do. After all, we've had a lot of coffees together over the years, haven't we?"

He went over to place their order. She sat there, quietly staring through the window and out at the community garden. *Why does he want to see me today? All those months when he never called me. Has he missed our friendship? Has he missed me?*

She looked at her watch. *Why am I wondering about the time? I've nothing else to do. I'm so nervous.*

He soon returned with their coffees, carefully placing them on the table.

"Oh, thank you." Picking up the mug, she placed it to her lips and sipped the coffee. *It's perfect. He remembered after all.*

He sat across from her at the small round table. "I suppose you're wondering why I called you."

"Well, I…"

He looked down at her coffee and then back up at her. "I hear you're doing extremely well in your singing…and that you are having a lot of gigs at church services, funerals and weddings."

"Yes, I guess I am. I seem to be in demand. It is very exciting to start a new career at my age. And the money sure helps to supplement my pension."

He sipped his coffee and then placed the mug back on the table. "You must especially enjoy the weddings."

"Yes, but I enjoy singing at church services and funerals as well." *What are you getting at? All the years* we were friends, you always avoided mentioning weddings or marriage. Did you know how much I would have liked to take our relationship beyond just a friendship?

He looked down at his watch as if to check the time.

"Do you have to go some place?"

"No. I'm sorry. I wasn't checking the time. I guess it's just a nervous habit."

"Why? Are you nervous?" she asked.

"Well there's something I wanted to tell you about and…well—"

"Come on now, this is me, we've known each other forever."

"Yes, you're right, I should be able to share anything with you."

She cupped her hands around the still warm mug of coffee. *What is he trying to tell me? I don't know what to expect. What's that my father always told me to do in these situations—'expect the best and prepare for the worst'.*

He looked her in the eyes and said, "I'm getting married."

So many thoughts were swirling around in her head. Her body went numb. She worked her best to gain composure. "Well…I…I'm delighted for you."

"Thank you. I knew you would be. You've always been such a dear friend."

She looked at her watch and said, "You know I must get going. Sorry I have to run. I don't know where the time has gone."

He looked surprised. "Before you go, there's something I wanted to ask you."

"Yes…yes, of course. What is it you want to ask me?"

"I wanted to know if you would sing at my wedding."

She sat there in a daze.

He took a drink of his coffee and then looked at her and said, "How's your coffee?"

"HOW'S MY COFFEE?"

Umberto
David Rasmussen

    The whole thing is really quite astounding.

    There I was, my life falling apart. No sooner had I lost my position with the firm, when my wife ran off and left me. It seemed that everyone—all my friends—had taken the position of supporting my wife in her leaving me, and my firm in dismissing me. They had all cast me aside, as if I were no longer worthy of their time.

    Sure, I wasn't an innocent party to what had transpired. Yes, I had been involved in a financial scandal. I remember, vividly, that day when the police came to my office and took me away in handcuffs. But it wasn't long before they realized I wasn't the only player—in fact, I was a very small fish. They wanted the big fish. If I were to give them up, the authorities would not only drop the charges against me, but also offer something so attractive I couldn't possibly refuse.

What I was given was the opportunity to begin a new life in another city—away from my ex-wife and my ex-friends. My parents were deceased. I had no siblings and no children. The Witness Protection Program would provide me with a new life, essentially without sacrifice.

I saw it all as an opportunity to reinvent myself. How many individuals get to do that in their mid-sixties? It all came together when I saw a photo of the Italian professor and writer, Umberto Eco. That's what I wanted for my new look! And so, I grew a beard, let my hair grow longer and replaced my contact lenses with eyeglasses.

Then there was that day when I drove into town to look at hats—hats that Umberto would wear. I took along a photo of him, complete with hat, into an exclusive men's apparel shop and said, "I want one like this."

I couldn't believe the time I had, standing in front of a full-length mirror, trying on hat after hat. A small crowd of men and women gathered around me. And then, the moment arrived when I looked in the mirror and knew I'd found the perfect one—a black fedora that framed my face and gave me an air of mystery. The bystanders actually applauded my choice.

Yes, this Witness Protection Program has given me a new lease on life. The special government pension allows me to enjoy a simple, yet exciting lifestyle. My new friends all call me Umberto. I'm even learning to speak Italian.

And I'm becoming something of a writer...

The Pump
David Rasmussen

I was awakened by voices. It was shift change in the Acute Care ward. In the darkness I began to piece it all together.

Morning…seven-thirty…Tuesday…my third day here.

I opened my eyes—though still not wanting to accept the fact that the day was beginning. I thought to myself, Could this be the day I go home?

I lay there in bed. Quiet had returned to my room. I could hear the tick…tick…tick…of the pump beside me as it pushed saline solution and antibiotics into my body.

In the darkened room I became aware of someone beside my bed. As I opened my eyes I heard a voice, "Good morning, Mr. Rasmussen…my name is…and I'll be your morning nurse." Then, after checking my IV pump, she disappeared—off to her next patient.

I closed my eyes and lay there thinking. It would seem that my role in all of this is simple enough…make that long trip to the washroom. But do I really want to go? I don't want to, but I guess I should.

And so I began my trek. I was the only one of the three patients in my room able to get out of bed. The man to my left and the woman to my right, both behind green curtains, had recently undergone surgery. Fortunately, I had avoided that fate.

I carefully climbed out of bed, thankful my lower abdominal pain was greatly reduced. I stood in front of the IV pump to which I was tethered. Rolling the unit towards me, I reached around behind it and unplugged it from the wall. The pump continued as ever, but now on battery power. I navigated myself and my IV unit through the labyrinth, around my bed and down the narrow corridor to the washroom.

I took care of my bladder, my first project of the day, and then made the return journey with the IV unit still in tow. As I plugged it back into the wall, I stopped to examine the unit. The electronic panel displayed the dosage, 125ml/hour, and the amount remaining, 417ml. It was then I noticed the large yellow label…'CHEMOTHERAPY PUMP'.

That's a bit strange. Perhaps it's from another department.

Seeing this 'chemotherapy pump' reminded me of a dear friend who had been in this hospital about a year ago. I had visited him every week for several months. We spoke 'of many things'.

Had he actually used this very same pump?

As I began to crawl back into my bed, I experienced some confusion over which direction my IV tube should take. But finally I worked it out. I was back in bed.

An empty bladder. Now I'm ready to take on the day.

Soon my meds arrived. The nurse smiled and said, "You can wait for your meal tray, before taking them."

My meal. I hope it's a lot better than yesterday's breakfast.

The IV alarms for the two patients on either side of me suddenly went off simultaneously.

Problem! Low IV solution? Pump stopped working? Air in line?

A few minutes later the room became quiet again. As promised, my meal arrived. Spread out in front of me was my breakfast tray. It looked suspiciously like all three meals I'd had the day before. The main course was lemon Jell-O.

After finishing my meal and remembering to take my meds, I sat there feeling somewhat satisfied. I wondered, Why am I not feeling hungry from this all-liquid diet? That's when I looked over at the IV pump as it continued to inject the saline solution into my body. I put on my glasses and read the large print on the bag. It contained 5% dextrose. The chemist in me began to work.

125ml/hour times 24 hours would be…that would be about three litres per day…at 5% sugar…Let's see…at 10% would be 300…so 5% would be 150… One hundred and fifty grams per day. No wonder I'm not hungry.

I wondered what time it was.

I'll have to get my cell phone out from that bedside table. Now that's a big deal. I'll have to lower the bed back down and reach over, being careful of my IV tube. Oh boy, this is a strain. There, now I have it. It's...9:44. Where has the time gone?

The rest of my day passed very well. I was feeling better by the hour. There were even moments when I actually thought to myself, Am I in a spa? I just lie here in bed and people bring me my meals. I have magazines and a newspaper to read. My main jobs continue to be taking my meds, eating my meals, staying attached to my IV machine and, of course, my visits to the toilet.

The two of us continued to make that trek every few hours. I was getting used to the drill. I was doing my part towards my recovery.

After lunch, where the main course was chicken broth, the surgeon arrived to give me the good news. I could go home today, after my 6:00 p.m. IV antibiotics.

Yes, I'm going home today.

My wife arrived in the afternoon and then the time went even faster. I had dinner—and it was no longer that all-liquid stuff. I was now into real food. A feast lay before me as I read the menu, BBQ Pork Rib, Prince Edward Medley, Rice Pilaf...

Eventually, my final antibiotic treatment was completed. The nurse separated me from the IV machine.

It was time to go. I got dressed and gathered up my things.

But I had one last thing to do. I walked around to the side of my bed. I gently touched the top of the 'chemotherapy pump' and said goodbye.

I felt blessed. I did get to go home from the hospital. Sadly, my friend never did.

Sidewalk Café
David Rasmussen

It was open house at our home in celebration of my wife's sixty-fifth birthday. I knew everyone there, except for one woman.

Donna turned to me. "David, I'm glad you can finally meet my friend, Marilyn."

"It's very nice to meet you, Marilyn. I've heard so much about you."

"It's very nice to meet you, David. But I must say, you're not at all what I expected."

I responded, "You know, I didn't expect to turn out this way either."

For one of the few times in my life, I was able to come up with what I felt was a brilliant response. It got a big laugh from Marilyn, as well as from my daughter-in-law who was seated nearby.

Since the event, my words, 'I didn't expect to turn out this way either', keep returning to my mind. What do these words say about me? What would Jung or Freud say about them? What if it was a Freudian slip? Did I just wake up after sleeping for fifty years and wonder, *How did I get here?*

My life has taken some unexpected turns over the years. I've had three, yes *three,* failed marriages. Sadly, I'm estranged from two of my four children. At age fifty I suffered a brain injury that affects me to this day. What other turning points did I encounter in my past? Maybe I don't need to recall any more. That should be enough for any man.

Would I have done things differently with what I know now? Yes, of course. Well, maybe. Probably not. Having suffered a brain injury, I've lost a great deal of my memories, good and bad. They were taken away from me, stolen late one night.

Perhaps, rather than dwelling on the paths I did or didn't follow and the decisions I did or didn't make, I should look on the events of the past as formative, making me just the way I am today. Yes, that's what's important. I can't go back and change the past. In fact, I believe I'm a better person because of all that has happened to me.

Recently, I've been experiencing some significant problems with my brain function. My doctor referred me to a psychiatrist. At the time, I was rather surprised about his decision, but now I see the value in it. The psychiatrist has diagnosed me as having a relapse of the post-traumatic stress disorder from my brain injury seventeen years ago. I'm being helped to deal with my brain function through therapy and medication. Another important aspect of my sessions is that the psychiatrist has become a window into who I am. I love the term she uses when referring to the problems in my past. She says I have led a *colourful* life. I like that. There is nothing negative in the word. As well, she continues to tell me how impressed she is with my ability to do the best I can with what I have.

Maybe that's what it's all about—to be the best that one can be. I've done my best to let go of the baggage I've encountered along the way. What I'm attempting to say is, I want to be the very best I can regardless of my past, my reduced brain function, and the fact that I can't do all the things I once did.

Actually, I can do things now that I never could before. I'm much more peaceful and calm, and I don't carry around the anger I once did. In recent years, I've taken up creative writing—something I never thought I could do.

Today is Thanksgiving Day. As I sit at a sidewalk café, on this sunny afternoon, I'm truly grateful for who I am now. It's been said, 'It's not the destination, but the journey'. But I say, it's not so much the journey I have travelled, but the destination I have reached—one of peaceful contentment.

Perhaps, at sixty-seven, I didn't expect to turn out this way, but I have arrived at where I want to be.

Writings from The Oval Table

Earth Day
David Rasmussen

I'm seated in my usual pew near the back of the small wooden church. It's Earth Day, and we are celebrating the four ancient elements—earth, air, fire, and water. The minister reminds the congregation of what our Earth provides for us—air to breathe, fire to warm us, water to drink.

What would I say if given the opportunity to speak today? My outdoor experiences of hiking, trekking and mountain climbing have taught me how to survive in remote places. The rule of threes applies—a person can survive for three weeks without food, three days without water, three hours without shelter and three minutes without air.

I'll never forget that day in Nepal…

I climbed one step at a time on the bare slope. The winds were so strong that, at times, I had trouble maintaining my balance. To make matters worse, they tried to steal what little breath I had. Fortunately, I wasn't alone in this inhospitable place. I had my Sherpa guide, Pisang, at my side.

Eventually, the slope levelled off. With some difficulty, I read my mountaineering watch: 4980 metres. I realized we had not yet achieved our goal. Prior to our departure, a detailed topographical map had shown a suitable objective on the ridge at 5043 metres.

I pointed to my watch and called out to Pisang, who was standing less than a metre away, "Not 5000."

Pisang had a puzzled look on his face.

As the wind buffeted against us, I pointed to my left and yelled, "Traverse." I momentarily lost my breath. "Climb higher."

Pisang turned and looked at the adjacent slope. Without discussion, we set off in that direction.

The wind did not lessen, nor did the sound of it whistling around us, but it didn't take long to complete the traverse and soon we were once again on an ascent.

I climbed one exhausting step at a time. My backpack grew heavier and heavier. I kept telling myself that my fifty-three-year-old body could make it. I concentrated on each individual step, something the Buddhists refer to as mindfulness. As I focused on each step, the cold, the winds, the shortness of breath, began to fade away.

Frigid winds greeted us at the top of the slope, trying their best to bring us to our knees. Pisang was a typical Sherpa, slight of build, short, but very strong. I was almost twice his weight and I wondered why he wasn't blown off the mountain.

Once again, I checked my watch for the ever-important altitude. 5050 metres—we had done it!

I soon realized our objective was more than just a level section on the ridge. A pile of large rocks held up a pole covered with dozens of prayer flags flapping in the wind. This was a place of significance to the Sherpa people.

I unzipped my mountaineering jacket very slightly. Zipping open the top of the heavy fleece layer underneath, I reached inside. My camera, which had been warm and snug all day, was now yanked out into the elements. My thick gloves made it difficult to adjust the camera settings and, if that wasn't bad enough, I could hardly see through my glacier glasses. Hoping I had the right settings, I photographed my climbing partner and he returned the favour.

My mind was taken back to what I had achieved. Only a week before, I had arrived on a large Russian helicopter, at the mountain village of Lukla. Since then, I'd trekked more than 50 kilometres through the Khumbu valley, the home of the Sherpa people for more than 400 years. In addition, I had become acclimatized by climbing up more than 2000 metres.

The wind brought me back to reality. I began to take in the spectacular panorama under the blue skies. Down the Imja Valley, far in the distance, was Dingboche, where we had departed early that morning. That gathering of stone huts was our only connection to the outside world. It was our lifeline—for shelter, for food, for water and for richer air. Across the valley loomed the great peak of Ama Dablam. Looking up the valley was Island Peak and behind it, a massive ridge of ice and snow. Peeking over the ridge was a treasure, my first view of Makalu, the fifth highest mountain on the planet.

Pisang and I then turned our backs away from the valley. Above us towered a wall of sheer rock, ice, and snow—the South Face of Lhoste, arguably the most difficult climb on earth. We were so close to the wall that we had to strain our necks as we looked higher and higher to eventually see the summit of the world's fourth highest peak, more than 3000 metres above us.

I was overcome by the magnitude of Lhoste. That was, until I realized what lay just beyond. I couldn't see her, but I could feel her presence. For behind this wall of rock, ice and snow was the mountain of all mountains—the very summit of Everest. The Sherpas call her Chomolungma, Mother Goddess of the World. To be in her presence was a deeply spiritual moment for me.

Although I was exhausted and cold, I was hesitant to leave. I would likely never again stand on this spot, for to visit it, even with the most modern and rapid means of travel, requires a journey of some three weeks. But Pisang and I knew it was time. We hugged each other and began our descent back to civilization, leaving behind a world of stark beauty, a world only to be visited for a brief moment in time.

A few minutes down the slope, Pisang found a small, but somewhat sheltered alcove in the rocks, where we rested and caught our breath. He reached into his backpack and removed a piece of yak cheese and some dried sausage. It was a privilege to share food and shelter with this young Buddhist.

Although we felt some comfort in our refuge we could not stay there for long. Even though I was becoming acclimatized to this very high altitude, it was still difficult to breathe. The air at 5000 metres is much thinner, almost half that of sea level. Without acclimatization, a person could not function in this rarefied air. If transported immediately from sea level to this spot, one could not survive, even three minutes, without falling unconscious. Soon after, death would occur.

Strengthened by the short rest, the simple meal, and a well-earned drink of water, we descended the windy slope where we finally reached the calm valley floor. We hiked across the barren land of dirt and gigantic boulders. At times I felt like an astronaut walking on the moon. In the late afternoon, after a nine-hour adventure, we reached Dingboche, where we found shelter from the winds, the warmth of a fire, some food and drink—

The minister's voice penetrates my thoughts. "So, let us always be grateful for our Mother Earth. Let us nurture her and protect her, for she provides us with everything we need."

A tear runs down my cheek.

I have been blessed with an appreciation of all we receive from our Earth, for I have journeyed to the very edge of earth, air, fire, and water.

Life's Sweet Moments
David Rasmussen

I'm not certain why he stood out in the crowd. Perhaps it was the bright red T-shirt against his dark complexion, or the fact that he appeared to be on his own, which seemed unusual, as he was likely no older than eight.

He was noticeably agitated as he approached me. "Excuse me, sir. Could you please help me?"

"Yes. What can I do for you?" I replied.

"I'm scared. I'm very scared."

"What's wrong?"

He pointed towards the supermarket's entrance. "That man. He looked at me. He scared me."

I put my arm around the boy and we walked towards the entrance. I guided him past the man, who was seated on a bench nearby, wearing a black baseball cap and sunglasses.

After entering the store, the young lad appeared to relax. He stopped, opened his hand, and said, "I have to buy some eggs. I have three dollars."

We headed off to the back of the store where we encountered a large assortment of eggs. He didn't seem to know which ones to select. I picked up a carton and opened it. "These are the ones I buy. Do you want them?"

"Yes. I have three dollars. Do I have enough?"

"You should have enough," I said.

On the way to the checkout, he thanked me repeatedly.

He presented the eggs to the cashier, who said, "That will be two ninety-nine."

The boy proudly opened his hand and gave her the three dollars.

She placed the carton of eggs in a plastic bag and handed it to him, along with the receipt.

"Don't I get any change?" he asked.

"Oh, no dear. There isn't any change."

As we walked out the door, I checked to see if the man was still there. Fortunately, he wasn't.

"Which way do you go home?" I asked.

He pointed towards the end of the block. "Over there at the red light."

As we walked along, I asked, "What's your name?"

"Mohammed."

"Well, it's very nice to meet you. I have a friend named Mohammed. My name is David."

We arrived at the intersection, where he confidently reached out and pushed the crosswalk button.

Eventually, the cars came to a complete stop and the walk light came on. Without saying a word, he began his journey across the six lanes of traffic.

I stood there and watched him carrying the plastic bag. Once safely on the far side of the street he turned and waved to me. I waved back. I felt a little sad to be saying goodbye to my new friend.

A moment later, he motioned with his hand. He did it once more.

Then I realized Mohammed was blowing me kisses.

Walking back to the supermarket to pick up the jug of milk I'd come for, I knew I had just experienced one of life's sweet moments.

Writings from The Oval Table

Anthology

Doreen Tadros

The Old Testament For Dummies
Part 1- The Beginning
Doreen Tadros

It all began the morning Adam woke with a pain in his side. He looked out at his beautiful garden that was filled with fruit-bearing trees and animals of all kinds. There, eating one of his apples, was a new creature. Since his dad had given him the job of naming all the creatures, he named her woman. (Later she told him she wanted to be called Eve.)

She offered him one of the apples. He refused, saying that his dad had told him not to eat the apples.

"At your age do you still do everything your dad tells you?" she asked as she re-offered the apple.

To prove himself a man, he took the apple and said, "Of course not."

The snake in the grass sneaked in the information that, if Adam ate the apple, he would be like the gods and know good from evil.

He ate the apple and immediately knew good. Good was standing in front of him. Sometime later he discovered evil; it was called a headache.

They moved out of the garden and lived together.

Eve thought that Adam wanted to spend too much time begetting, so she insisted that they both wear a fig leaf to remind Adam to get another hobby. This just confused Adam and was the beginning of men's conflict between what their indoctrinated brains told them was right and what was beneath that damn fig leaf.

Meanwhile, Eve spent much of her time, when she wasn't looking after her increasing brood, making grass skirts out of the local bulrushes, and bangles and rings out of clay.

Adam pointed out that she only needed one skirt, which earned him time with the dog, there being no dog houses in that era.

Eve's obsession with clothing and jewellery was the beginning of women's obsession with those items. This was later brought to heights Eve could never have imagined, with the emergence of Dior and the French fashion houses. Later, the Americans, realizing the financial benefits, muscled in on the commerce and made all women feel inadequate unless they were wearing the latest fashion-tag on their rear ends.

A few generations later, eight of Eve's descendants were invited to go along on a boat ride with a chap called Noah. He told them they could bring along a few of their pets. He insisted that they bring a male and female of each kind of creature. It was a very large boat and everybody got along fine, even though it was pretty crowded, what with people, animals, birds, insects and piles and piles of food. There were boxes full of all sorts of diseases that would be needed later, even though nobody knew why at the time. It rained and rained but eventually they found dry land. They settled down and got on with their jobs of begetting.

Later generations of God's chosen people were enslaved in Egypt and God chose Moses to free them and lead them to the Promised Land. With God's help, Moses did a pretty good job of getting them out of Egypt but when he reached the wilderness, he hadn't a clue how to find the Promised Land.

At this point he had a choice, either ask God to show him the way, or just keep walking around looking for it. If he had asked directions, God would probably have stamped great big footprints in the sand for him to follow. (Rather like Ikea does in its stores today.) But Moses chose to find the way by himself. He just walked around, followed by the thousands of people he was leading. Finally, after forty years, he did find the Promised Land, by which time everybody was cranky and fed up.

Unfortunately, this gene that makes men think that they never need to ask directions, was passed on to all future generations of males, to which most women today can attest.

The Bible also says that the sins of the fathers shall be visited on the children: so, between their sins and their genes, we can safely say that nothing is our fault.

That's the Old Testament as I understand it.

A Night of Wonder
Doreen Tadros

Dressing in his red suit and hat, he adjusted his belt—one notch looser than last year. Santa was getting ready for his big night. The elves prepared his sleigh, filling it with a huge sack of toys. The reindeer were waiting, somewhat impatiently, to get going. Santa however was tired. He wasn't sure if he could carry out all his duties tonight.

The elves were worried. Then one of them had an idea. Two elves would ride with Santa and they would all take turns delivering toys down the various chimneys. They would be finished much sooner and Santa wouldn't be so tired. Santa was pleased with the idea, so they set out together happy and smiling.

All went smoothly until the very last house. Santa was part-way down the chimney when he became stuck. His belt was caught on a loose brick that was sticking out inside the chimney. This had never happened to him before and he didn't know what to do. As he hung there, he rued the fact that he'd gained a few pounds... most of it around his middle.

Luckily the two elves were with him this year. When they peered over the edge of the chimney, they realized Santa's dilemma.

Quickly they went to work to free him. They pulled the string out from the neck of the now empty toy sack, then they dropped one end of the string down the chimney and tied the other end to the sleigh. Santa tied his end to his belt, then the reindeer pulled and pulled.

Soon Santa's belt popped open and Santa free-fell down the chimney, landing with a loud thud that winded him. As he lay there, he heard footsteps. It was the children's father, who had heard the thud and come down to investigate.

The two of them stared at each other, both in disbelief.

The father spoke first, "I didn't think you were real.... I always drink the milk and eat the cookie before the kids wake up. You never do."

"Well, now you know I'm real," replied Santa gruffly as he stood and dusted himself off. Then he picked up his belt and adjusted his buckle saying,

"Do you really think I can drink all that milk and eat all those cookie treats? Anyway, what I'd really like is a tot of rum!"

Father obliged, poring a rum and coke for each of them. Then they sat together, in the middle of the night, talking softly so as not to wake the sleeping household.

Eventually Santa felt revived. He picked up the toys from the hearth where they had fallen, placing them lovingly under the tree.

Then he turned abruptly to father and said, "Goodnight." Scared to go up the chimney, lest he got stuck again, he boldly walked out the front door.

The commotion had awakened the mother, who came downstairs and was surprised to find her husband standing outside in the snow, wearing only his pajamas, gazing skyward.

She led him inside and sat him down. Still dazed, he told her everything that had happened.

"There, there dear. You had a very tiring day getting everything ready for tomorrow. And that was a very heavy dinner, and maybe you had a little too much wine. Let's get you back to bed to get a bit more sleep. I'm sure you'll feel better in the morning."

As they passed by the living room, neither of them noticed the two empty glasses sitting on the coffee table.

The Girl Who Climbed the Mighty Oak and Caused Her Mother's Downfall
Doreen Tadros

    Josephine, Jo to her friends and everybody else who didn't want a fight, was nearly seven years old and was a tough little tomboy. Most of her days were spent in jeans or shorts and a tee-shirt playing with the local boys. They climbed trees, splashed in puddles or dug up worms and went fishing. She always came home dirty and was made to take a bath before she was allowed to sit or eat dinner. On the rare occasions when she wore a skirt, her mother was constantly admonishing her to sit with her knees together like a lady, or to pull down the hem of her skirt so that her knickers didn't show. (Here the mother showed her English heritage by calling them knickers instead of panties.)
    Jo had a sister, Patti, who was eight. She was everything her mother had hoped for in a daughter; clean, tidy, studious and girly. She preferred to play with dolls

or draw pictures than to do all the gross "boy" things that her sister enjoyed.

One day, when the girls arrived home from school, their mother said, "I'd like you to go and wash up and change into pretty dresses suitable to go out to a nice restaurant for dinner with Daddy."

It was only 3:30 but she wanted them to get ready straight away so that their dad could have a shower once he arrived home from work. They both did as they were told, although Jo did so reluctantly. Once they were dressed they both looked lovely. Mother was pleased.

"Now go and play quietly for an hour or so," she said.

"Let's play Barbies," Patti cried hopefully.

To Patti's surprise, Jo readily agreed as she ran off, saying she'd get her Ken doll.

She soon returned gripping a radically altered Ken. He had been stripped bare. Designs had been painted over his face and torso and feathers were glued to his head. "He's an Indian Brave with war paint," she announced. He did look brave and manly. (At least, he did from the waist up.)

Patti's face fell. This was not going as well as she'd hoped. She was dreading what was inevitably coming.

Holding Ken out in front of her, Jo made whooping sounds as she and Ken raced across the floor and grabbed Patti's pretty blond Barbie. Jo and Ken quickly lashed Barbie to the kitchen chair leg. Then, picking up a paring knife from the counter, they danced and whooped around the chair where Barbie stood awaiting her fate.

Suddenly they stopped. Ken, helped by Jo, took the knife and scalped the hapless Barbie, right there on the kitchen floor.

Patti was crying when Mom came, too late, to the rescue. Mom surveyed the debacle in front of her and banished Ken and Jo to the garden.

Jo, realizing she was in trouble, but not understanding why, made her way down the garden to her favorite tree to sulk.

Meanwhile, Patti looked out the window and saw Jo heading toward the big Oak. Four local boys were out there too. Patti started plotting her revenge. She knew Jo would be in big trouble if she climbed the tree in her best clothes.

Once Jo was inside the tree house, Patti yelled, "Mom, Jo has climbed up to the tree house in her best dress."

Mom went toward the back door, calling out to Jo. She looked out in horror just in time to see four little boys staring up at Jo as she climbed down.

"Come here at once Jo." She tried to stay calm.

The boys, recognizing trouble brewing, quickly disappeared.

"Jo, I've told you many times not to climb trees in a skirt and not to let the boys see your knickers. You just don't listen."

"But I did listen Mom, I didn't let them see my knickers. I took them off before I climbed up—see, they are in my pocket."

Jo was proud of herself.

Mother was horrified. Close to fainting, she propped herself against the tree, no longer knowing what to do or say but strongly believing that Jo had shamed the entire family.

Over the years many of the parents in the neighborhood had jokingly questioned whether Jo was really a boy.

Now, there were four little boys who knew the true answer to that question.

Writings from The Oval Table

Anthology

Karen Shaw

The Cowards
Karen Shaw

"Mommy! Mommy!" cried The Little Ones as they burst through the cabin door. "The Big Boys are throwing rocks at us and calling us names!"

Drying their tears, The Mother responded, "Sit down, My Little Ones. No matter where you go in this tiny northern village or in the biggest city, there will always be Bullies. I cannot always be with you. Listen carefully, here's what you must do. Always stick together. Stick up for each other. Never cry. Never, never let them know you're afraid. Remember to hold your head up and keep calm. You have to go right back out there and let them know they can't push you around."

The Little Ones returned outside and decided to visit their friend at the end of the block. Halfway down the road they were surrounded by the Pack of Bullies.

"Back for more?" The Bullies' Leader sneered.

"The Cry Babies are back!" his Brother teased. "Did you run to your mommy?" another bully challenged.

One Little One reached out and took the Other's hand.

"We want to see you run again. Run Cry Babies! Run Cry Babies!" the gang chanted.

Suddenly, a stone whizzed through the air and grazed a Little One's arm. Hot tears welled up in the Little One's eyes. The grip was tightened on the Other's hand. Together, with measured steps, they held their heads up and continued down the road.

"Aw! You're no fun!" The Leader spat. "Let's find some other cry babies."

Buoyed by their victory, The Little Ones returned home to recount the incident to Their Mother.

Still, the terrorism continued. The Big Boys would attack the Little Ones but whenever The Little Ones stuck together and stood their ground, The Bullies gave up.

After one such encounter The Little Ones decided to ask the Leader's Mother for help. They plucked up their courage and knocked on her door. When the door was opened, a snarling dog stood beside The Woman.

"You have Bad Boys!" The Little Ones blurted.

Before they could continue, The Mother threw back her head and roared with laughter. "I let My Boys fight their own battles!" she shouted. "Now get out of here you, You Conniving Little Tattletales or I'll sic my dog on you!"

Totally defeated, The Little Ones retreated down the stairs. They could hear The Mother still cackling and the dog barking as they raced home.

When The Little Ones started school, the attacks got worse. Because there were few hours of daylight in the little northern village, the children had to walk home in pitch darkness. Choosing a new site each time, The Bullies would ambush and beat up any younger children who happened by.

When The Little Ones urged Their Mother to walk them home from school, she answered, "I can't do that. I have to make supper. You're not babies anymore."

When they pleaded with Their Father, he replied, "I can't do that. I can't leave my work. You're old enough to stick up for yourselves."

When they begged Their Teacher, she responded, "I can't do that. I have to finish my work and prepare for tomorrow. Once you leave the school grounds, you aren't my responsibility."

"We'll wait for you. We'll sit so quietly and read. You'll never know we're here. Besides, you go right by our place," they tried again.

"No. If I make an exception for you, I'll end up babysitting the whole town! Run along like the rest of The Kids," The teacher demanded.

The Little Ones had no choice but to brave The Darkness and Whatever else lurked there.

"Help! Help!" The Little Ones screamed as they burst into the cabin. "The Big Boys…" There was no need to explain. While blood gushed from One's nose, The Other's black eye was quickly swelling shut.

Immediately, The Mother began first aid.

"Where are your jackets? And your boots?" she asked. "Where did this happen?"

Listening for the answer while he donned his parka and snow gear, without a word, The Father grabbed a flashlight and headed into the darkness and howling snow.

When he returned with their winter apparel, the freshly bathed Little Ones were bundled in layers of blankets and nursing their wounds with cups of steaming cocoa.

"I am so sorry, My Little Ones," The Father said through tears. "I feel I've let you down. I never wanted My Children to be fighters. I'd hoped you'd learn better ways to settle your childish squabbles." The Father took a deep breath and cleared his throat before continuing.

"...but taking your coats and making you walk home barefoot is going too far! You don't have to take this anymore. Here's what you must do." Both Little Ones listened intently.

"You already know about sticking together; now you have to learn to fight back. The next time Those Boys threaten you, look around and pick up the closest thing. It can be a rock, or a stick…whatever. Wave it over your head and say in your bravest voice, 'You come one step closer and I'll hit you with this!' Those Bullies might test you. Once you've given the challenge you can't change your mind or they'll beat you up worse than ever and never let you forget it! You have to carry through with your threat."

A few days later as The Little Ones returned from school, The Bullies surrounded them. "Back for more?" The Leader sneered.

The Little Ones looked around. There were no rocks. There were no sticks. Everything was covered in a deep layer of snow! One Little One spotted a Coke bottle and immediately seized it. Flinging it high overhead, The Little One exclaimed, "You take one step closer and I'll crack this over your head! Who wants to be first?"

"You grab the bottle," The Leader ordered His Brother.

"Not me! You get it!" The Brother protested.

Each of the gang echoed The Brother's response as one by one they disappeared.

Flinging the Coke bottle high overhead once more, The Little Ones re-enacted the incident for Their Parents at supper. The Mother laughed. The Father cheered when he heard how each Bully refused to follow Their Leader.

There was a sharp knock at the door before The Boys' Dad stormed into the cabin.

"What's this I hear about Your Kids going after My Boys with a broken beer bottle?!" he blurted. "I demand you put a stop to this immediately!" he hurled at The Father.

"A broken beer bottle?" The Father questioned. "Would you like to see it?"

At Their Father's request, The Little Ones reluctantly acted out the scenario again.

Noticing the black eye, bruises and cuts, The Boys' Dad asked for details.

"Your Sons have been terrorizing My Children for years. When they made them walk home barefoot without their jackets the other night I realized it was time for a change. I've decided to let My Kids fight their own battles."

New anger flared in The Boys' Dad's eyes as he swallowed hard. "My Boys won't give you any more trouble," he promised as he returned to the night.

Watching The Man disappear, The Father turned back to the supper table. "My Children, I am so proud of you! Do you see what your courage has done? I could have stuck up for you but Those Boys would have just waited until my back was turned. Did you notice they couldn't tell Their Dad the truth? They invented the broken beer bottle rather than admit their fear. All bullies are cowards." Taking The Little Ones in his arms he repeated, "Yes, I am so proud of you, My Daughters, so proud."

The Scrip
Karen Shaw

Festus, centurion in Caesar's army and homesick son,

To Lucius, my dear father:

What is it about farm boys? Instead of building highways or fighting battles for the emperor, I'm stuck preparing the food for the troops! Marching, cooking and cleaning make up most of my days—and nights for that matter. I'm not the first soldier to wish there was a way out of this routine. What was I thinking when I answered the conscription last fall? All I ever wanted was to be home with you for the harvest.

A few weeks ago I thought the gods had smiled on me. I found a scrip containing several months wages. My ticket home, I told myself. Now I could bribe people to keep quiet as I escaped. The idea lasted only a moment before a pang of conscience gripped me. I turned the purse over to Urbana, my captain. Good thing. It was his wallet! Next thing I knew Urbana was praising me in front of the troops!

"I like you, Festus," the captain said later. "You tell it like it is. You have a positive influence on the others. And you read and write? You could go far."

A week later, Urbana's signet ring was stolen from his tent. Enraged at the theft, he ordered the troops to be searched. To my astonishment, the captain ordered the guards to pass me by. "You've already proven yourself, soldier," he acknowledged as they went on to the next man. I won't tell you the fate of the thief. Let's just say I learned to never mess with the Roman army.

Within the month Urbana recommended me, and I was promoted to apprentice as member of the official guard to become a centurion. I will spare you the gruesome details of what all this entails, but suffice it to say that I have become an expert in the execution of convicted criminals. It is actually a high honour, and I am among the best although it does not always fit well with my heart.

What a strange country is this Israel, and the religion even stranger. Unlike us, the Jews have just one god, one who demands blood sacrifices. This is the end of Passover, a celebration that goes way back in their history but one they observe to the last ritual. Something about a lamb being offered for the people so they could avoid death.

Strange people too. There is always one leader or another trying to incite the people to overthrow Rome. It keeps us on our toes.

Or, there is Jesus, a man with the most unusual gifts. They say he heals people, even raises some from the dead. Just last month he called up a man named Lazarus. Everyone is still talking about it. Makes ya' wonder, eh? Jesus is always talking about a kingdom not of this world and about loving and forgiving each other. Such teaching is contrary to human nature.

    I finally got to see this teacher last week. Seemed harmless enough to me. His followers treated him like a king but the priests and officials were out to get him. He was apprehended one evening and put through several trials. The witnesses against him couldn't get their statements to agree. Finally, the priests cooked up some charge of blasphemy. Caiaphas, the high priest this year, claimed it would be good to have one man die for the people. What's with this blood sacrifice thing again?

    Because the priests were determined to have him executed, they needed the governor's approval. Not finding any fault with Jesus, Pilate wanted to release him. Citing his claims of a kingdom, the priests persuaded the governor that Jesus was worthy of death. Pilate finally gave in to their pressure. He turned Jesus over to the soldiers to be crucified. I was horrified.

    Until then, every person sentenced to death was an obvious criminal, fully deserving of the appointed sentence. However, on this day, a seemingly innocent man was sent to the cross.

    It was supposed to be my day off but I was assigned to stand guard during the execution. I was not pleased.

    I still can't believe what I heard. After being beaten, humiliated and crucified, this same Jesus actually looked out over the crowd and said, "Father, forgive them. They don't know what they are doing."

Forgive them? What was he thinking? In all that pain, knowing death was not far away, he spoke of forgiveness!

After about three hours it got really dark even though it was mid-day. I offered him vinegar several hours later. That's when things went very strange very fast. Within minutes, Jesus gave a loud cry that must have been his last breath. Immediately the earth shook. I learned later that the quake opened tombs and people actually were raised back to life. At the same moment, the curtain in their temple was ripped from top to bottom. Some say that was humanly impossible and must have been a divine hand opening the way for people to approach God. All I know is that I was terrified! "Surely, this man was the Son of God!" I found myself exclaiming.

At the priests' request, Urbana ordered the criminals' legs broken to hasten their deaths.

"There's no need for that here, Captain," I said. "This man is already dead."

"How can you be sure?" Urbana asked.

I thrust my spear into his side and was puzzled when blood and water gushed out of the same wound. Even on the farm, I know that is not natural. "Maybe he died of a broken heart," I offered.

I watched as they lowered Jesus' body and removed him from the cross. One thing about being a centurion, I know a dead body when I see one. Close up, there was absolutely no doubt. I watched his loved ones wrap him for the grave.

Before supper the next day, Urbana summoned me. "There's a rumor that Jesus' followers might try to steal his body in the middle of the night. Pilate wants sentries posted. Since I need someone I can trust, I'm putting you in charge. Take Maximo, Junio and Demas with you. Secure the tomb." Handing me his signet ring, he added, "Put this seal on the stone and stand guard all night."

Staying up all night with the sheep back home prepared me for the long night. No one got past me or the others.

Just before dawn on Sunday there was another earthquake. At the same moment, an angel moved the stone away from the tomb's entrance. How often have you seen an angel? We were so afraid we thought we'd die! Actually, we fainted.

By the time I recovered, I realized I was the last soldier there. I found out later the others ran straight to the priests and were bribed to make up a story. When I got to my feet, I swear I saw Jesus talking to a woman. He looked like he did last week—strong and whole, not like someone who had been through an ordeal; certainly not like someone who was dead. He was no ghost! It took me a few moments to comprehend that he actually did rise from the dead. He raised others and now he, himself, had risen. What did that have to do with me? I overheard him saying something about his going ahead to Galilee and having his followers meet him there.

I found my legs and raced to tell Urbana exactly what I'd experienced. "If anyone else told me that, I'd never have believed them. I have no reason to doubt you." After a pause, he continued, "You've earned an early discharge. How'd you like to be home for harvest? I'm being posted to Caesarea. I could use an aide like you.

Are you interested in the promotion until your discharge papers come through?"

And that is my story, Papa. Between my discharge and coming home in a few months, I'm going to Galilee to sort out these events and learn the teachings of Jesus. What happened today is going to sweep the world. I want to come home to prepare my little Roman village. I believe the power of one man to conquer death will change many lives, even mine.

Give my love to Mother. Tell her I miss her almost as much as I miss her home cooking.

I hope receiving this scroll with Urbana's seal was not a great shock to you. The captain ordered my message be sent by special envoy.

In a strange, indirect way, it looks like that scrip was my ticket home after all.

Sharon and the Ball of String
Karen Shaw

When Sharon was four years old she lived in a little house in the tiny Yukon village of Mayo Landing, between Dawson City and Keno. Her house had three rooms, each separated by a passageway without doors to allow heat to circulate freely from the kitchen stove. From the center of each ceiling, a bare light bulb was suspended. The lights were turned on or off by pulling on the cord attached to the bulb's chain.

The kitchen was the largest room in the house and boasted a green water pump, the only indoor plumbing. Each morning the pump was primed and cold water would be placed in kettles and basins on the huge wood stove to heat for food preparation, cleaning and bathing. In the center of the room were a roughly hewn table and an assortment of chairs.

A large over-stuffed couch and matching chair dominated the living room. Against one wall rested a four-foot tall radio that provided the latest tunes from

Seattle and mysterious language programs from Europe. Beside the radio stood Budgie's cage. Various framed pictures were scattered against the walls.

In the bedroom Sharon and I slept on the top of an enormous bunk bed while our parents occupied the lower bunk. Under the foot of the bed was a covered commode, sometimes known as a chamber pot, a potty, or, as some folks called it, a gazzunder (because it "goes under" the bed). Since there was no indoor plumbing except the kitchen pump, this is what was used to answer the call of nature. Several times a day, and certainly the last thing at night, our mother would dump the contents appropriately and clean the vessel.

Our dad was the fire chief. When the weather was particularly cold he had to stay the night at the fire hall to ensure the hoses and water lines didn't freeze. The night of this story was just such a night.

"I've already explained to you girls that I have to go to the doctor tonight," Mom told us again. "I tried to see him earlier but he was making his rounds at one of the mining towns."

Sharon and I protested. We had never been left alone before.

"No one is available to babysit. You will be fine on your own. Just remember three rules: No fighting. No playing with the fire. Don't let any strangers in the house." Pointing to the table, she continued, "I've left a snack. When you're hungry, help yourself. When you're tired, go to bed. You'll be fine." With that she passed out the hugs and kisses and crunched her way through the snow to her appointment.

Bored with her toys, Sharon spied a huge ball of stout butcher's twine on the counter. Holding the ball in her hands she wondered how long the string was. She wondered how many knots she could tie. Slowly she began to unwind the ball. With one end free, she tied a knot around a chair, then the table leg. So far so good, she thought to herself, now around the foot of the stove. Sharon realized she could loop the string and pull the ball through. It was even easier than tying a knot! She looped the sturdy string through the handles of the oven door, frying pan, coal scuttle, wood box, around the green pump, encircled the door handle, through the handle of the cutlery drawer, and back around the table leg.

She jumped up onto the table and wound the string around the light bulb and then, for good measure, back around the door handle. After everything in the kitchen was firmly secured, she continued the ball of string to the living room and wound it around the knob on the radio, back to the couch, around Budgie's cage, about each picture, and so it wouldn't feel left out, once around the other radio knob before tackling the bedroom.

Coincidentally the string ran out at the same time as Sharon's imagination did. With nothing left to do, Sharon crawled into bed and fell sound asleep.

What Sharon didn't know, and wouldn't have understood if she had been told, was that our dear mother was suffering from a bladder infection. By the time Mom walked home from the doctor she had only one thing on her mind. Thankful to be at the house, she turned the door handle. The door would not open.

She knocked. She called. She banged and kicked and screamed and hollered and pounded and cried but no one opened the door. Finally she hurled her entire body weight against the door. It opened a smidgen—just enough for her to catch a glimpse of the interior. With awesome dexterity she unwound the string attached to the door and was able to squeeze through the opening.

A three-dimensional maze challenged her. Not only was picking her way across the floor like a walk through a minefield, she had to maneuver through a giant cobweb, unsure which strand was attached to a breakable object. With acrobatic skill she worked her way to the bedroom.

Reaching under the bed for the chamber pot she took a firm grip of the handle and pulled the object towards herself. It wouldn't move! She tugged again. It wouldn't budge! She tore the mattress off her bed to discover the gazzunder and lid were securely fastened to the bedsprings! In desperation, she found that super-human strength reserved only for child protection and bladder infections, ripped the pot from the springs and took care of the business at hand.

Relieved and composed at last, she looked up at her children who were dreaming the dreams of the innocent.

The priming of the pump signaled morning and time to get up. Sleepy-eyed, Sharon wandered into the kitchen. "So, where's all the string?" she asked.

"It's been put away," Mom answered.

"But where?" Sharon asked again.

"Away," Mom replied and Sharon knew from her tone of voice that Mom would never reveal the hiding place.

"Are you the one that played with the string last night?" Mom inquired.

"Yes. I wanted to see how long a ball of string was," Sharon answered.

"How long is it?" Mom asked.

"Three rooms long. And, I wanted to see how many knots I could tie."

"How many?"

"I don't know. I get mixed up after thirteen." Sharon replied. "And, I wanted to keep the strangers out."

"Well, you certainly succeeded there!" Mom laughed.

Our parents wisely decided that Sharon would not be punished for her escapade. She meant no harm. She had an insatiable curiosity. And, after all, she had obeyed The Rules! Even so, neither of us was ever again allowed to play with string.

Years later when Sharon had children of her own, she discovered again just how long a ball of string could be. She learned multitudinous knots. She took up macramé and learned that each knot had its own name, each one beautiful. No one ever hid the string from her again.

The Flood
Karen Shaw

Leaning on her cane, Betty Triplow stands on the train tracks watching the tide recede for the second time that day. She is numb as she observes the devastation surrounding her. The waves, now chocolate brown, suck more earth back into the bay with each lap. Excavators still remove trees, mud and other debris from the tracks. To her left, Betty observes traces of mud as far east as the train station while the high water mark rises halfway up Coldicutt Hill to her right. The water marks on the cottages along her Marine Drive neighbourhood are above four feet.

Memories rush through Betty's mind. She recalls the railway shunting grounds which once occupied the spot where she stands. The picnic tables behind her fill the space where a string of small units, The Semiahmoo Cabins, stood until the mid-sixties.

With the excitement of the day, Betty has abandoned her regular routine. She recalls being awakened by thunder claps. Limping to the window she watched a great funnel cloud move from the bay to hover over the city. Hail bounced off the roads and covered the sandbars on the outgoing tide. When the hail switched to rain, the deluge caused the manhole covers to jump six feet into the air. The overwhelming volume of water slammed against the hillside sweeping away Duprez' Ravine. The mudslide ripped a dozen trees out by the roots.

She had skipped breakfast and lunch. Her tummy tells her it is time for supper but she lingers on the tracks. She muses how the papers might record today's storm and imagines the headlines, "June 8, 1999—Water Spouts Wreak Havoc on Seaside City". She wonders how many others witnessed the funnel clouds. With all the power lines down around her place she has not been able to keep up with the TV reports. All day she has relied on neighbours to keep her informed.

"Believe me, Betty," Letitia assured her. "All the schools have been closed. Even Semiahmoo Mall was evacuated. Apparently, the wiring is in the floor and the dentists were worried a patient might be electrocuted."

Her eyes sweep across Semiahmoo Bay as she scans the horizon against the San Juan Islands. A young couple walking hand in hand catches Betty's eye. She remembers walking the beach with Martin. A sudden chill grips her when she realizes that it was exactly fifty-nine years to the day when she last saw him.

Her mind floats back to that day in 1940. His army uniform made Martin look handsome and professional. Newly enlisted, he had been granted leave to bid farewell to his loved ones before boarding the train in New Westminster for active service. Earlier that morning as they strolled along the sand, they made plans for their future.

"Promise me you'll wait for me, Betty. This war can't last forever."

"Of course, I'll wait for you. There'll never be anyone else."

Betty handed him a small package wrapped in oilcloth. "Here, Marty, take this. It's a little Bible. Please, carry it over your heart. See my note inside the front cover. *Darling Marty, You will be in my heart forever. Love, Betty.*" She laughed as she added, "I even put my address there as a reminder to write me."

The couple returned to her family's cottage where Betty began packing Martin's lunch. As she wrapped the tuna sandwiches, her brother, Joe, stomped into the kitchen.

"Smells good," Joe grunted. "Where's mine?"

"Your lunch will be ready soon," Betty assured him. "We have wonderful news. Martin has asked me to marry him when he gets back from the war. There's no ring yet but we're engaged!"

Joe's face purpled as he grabbed Martin's collar. "Wudda'ya mean comin' here and takin' my sister away? Who's gonna' do the work around here when she's gone? You don't expect me to keep this farm runnin' on my own, do ya'?" At that, the bully turned on his heels and skulked off into the forested hillside behind their place.

"I'm sorry, Martin. My brother is always flying off the handle. I guess he never thought I'd leave." Betty handed Martin the bagged lunch. "Did you say you were meeting the other enlisted men along North Bluff for a ride into

New Westminster? Better hurry. You don't want to miss them. Take the short cut through Duprez' Ravine."

Martin gathered his gear, embraced Betty and quickly kissed her before disappearing up the steep trail behind her house.

There was confusion in the days that followed. Martin had not reported for duty; in fact, he never met up with the other soldiers along North Bluff. Joe told the investigators he watched the soldier double back and hide in a southbound freight car.

At first, Betty wouldn't believe Joe's account. "It's just not like Martin to do that. He was proud to serve his country. Besides, we had plans."

"Forget about him," Joe snorted. "You'll never see that no good deserter again."

Long after the war had ended, Betty waited for Martin's return. Finally, she resigned herself to life without him. She cared for her aging father and helped Joe farm their plot of land at the water's edge.

A few years after Martin's disappearance, Joe married Syl. His marriage didn't change him. His moods and cruelty were predictable. When Syl's parents died, she sold her parents' property and fled before Joe could spend her inheritance. Betty often wished she had escaped with Syl. When Joe died of a massive heart attack, she was left on her own.

Betty is zapped back to the present when someone taps her arm. After a moment she recognizes her off-duty postman.

"Excuse me, Miss Triplow, these RCMP officers asked me to find you."

"Me? Why me? What's this all about?" Betty asks.

One officer gestures to a picnic table where his partner waits. "Let's sit down. We need to talk."

"We understand you knew Martin Offner," the first officer begins.

"Martin Offner? What has he got to do with today? He was my fiancé but he disappeared exactly fifty-nine years ago."

"Miss Triplow, the landslide uncovered a body from the ravine. There wasn't much left except army ID and a Bible wrapped in oilcloth. We believe they belonged to Offner."

"Martin? Couldn't be," Betty gasps. When she catches her breath she continues, "What happened? Did he fall? Hit his head? Break his neck?"

"Stabbed in the back, I'm sorry to say."

The mountie shows her a plastic bag containing a hunting knife. " Would you mind looking at this knife? Perhaps you could identify it."

Betty hesitates. Her heart pounds, "It's...it's my brother's knife. I had it especially engraved for him," she begins to sob. "See, the handle reads 'JT' for Joseph Triplow. I gave it to him the Christmas before Martin left."

Betty hides her face in her hands as tears flood down her face. Finally, she knows the truth.

Writings from The Oval Table

Anthology

Robert Ramsay

A Sloppy Time on the High Iron
Robert Ramsay

"We're in for a sloppy time on the high iron tonight," Louis said, handing me another stack of clean tablecloths to stash in the locker.

"Why do you say that?" I asked.

It was the summer of 1966. I'd been hired by Canadian National Railway as a waiter on the *Super Continental*, and Louis Gauthier, the dining car steward, was giving me last minute instructions before the train left Winnipeg.

"We're three hours late, Bob," Louis explained. "The front end will want to make up time, so be prepared for some fast running as soon as we get out of town. This dining car will be rockin' and rollin', so take a good long look at these snowy white tablecloths. They'll soon be soaked with coffee, soup and gravy."

I was placing vases on the tables—one red, one white carnation—when the dining car leapt forward and we rolled out of the train shed.

"Must be Stampede Mike at the throttle," Louis said.

"How can you tell who the engineer is?"

"Stampede Mike handles the throttle like he's chasing wild broncos. He'll have it in notch 8 sooner than a gandy dancer can pound a spike. Luckily we've got the Sceneramic dome car behind us. Its weight will dampen some of the movement, but I'd better teach you how to avoid dumping meals onto some unlucky diner's lap."

He showed me how to keep my knees slightly bent to absorb some of the motion when I walked, and to surreptitiously snug my thigh against a table when taking orders or handing out plates. "Just take it slow this first evening," he said. "You'll soon get the hang of moving *with* the train instead of *against* it."

Louis glanced at his watch. "Thirty minutes until the cattle show up for dinner, so we'd better shove our throttles into notch 8 too. Finish with those vases and then start laying the tables. One more piece of advice. There'll be at least one ornery old cow or bad-tempered bull at every seating. Be polite and remember that it'll only be an hour before he or she'll be gone back to their sleeper."

There were five waiters and Louis to serve forty diners, so I knew I'd have to hustle. I'd barely finished laying the tables when the cattle started bunching up in the vestibule, waiting to be seated. I stifled a laugh. They really did look like the cows at milking time on my grandparents' farm—poking their faces through the fence, pawing the ground, anticipating their evening ration of chopped oats and sweet hay.

As Louis seated the cattle, I moved down one side of the aisle with the water pitcher. My task was to fill water glasses, hand folks the menus, and instruct them to write their choices on the order slips kept in the holder next to the salt and pepper shakers.

By this time we were out of the city and Stampede Mike was living up to his name. If the Sceneramic dome car was smoothing out the motion, it was news to me. The dining car was behaving like a crazily balanced teeter-totter. It rocked from side to side while the ends yawed back and forth. Each time the train passed over a road crossing, the car rose slightly before plunging down again. Besides the motion, the noise made concentration difficult—the howl of steel wheels on steel rails, mysterious squeaks, groans and rattles. It sounded and felt like we were serving dinner on top of a rumbling volcano.

I willed my muscles to move with the train instead of fighting its wild motion. Still, I over-filled a few water glasses, but the diners were good sports. One elderly gentleman even complimented me on being able to pour anything when travelling at such a high speed.

The last table was occupied by a family of three, leaving one place vacant. I had finished pouring their water, without spilling a drop, when the door opened. Ushered in by the clickety-clack roar of the rails, came someone I had no desire to see—Miss Gladys Brumutt, or as we twelfth graders had christened her, Glad Ass Mutt, our French teacher.

She was a graduate of what must have been the Gestapo Normal School. She took delight in boxing our ears if we didn't ape her words exactly. She was wearing her usual costume: a black, pleated skirt and a frilly white blouse. On her head she sported a wide-brimmed straw hat decorated with pheasant feathers. A cloud of lavender-scented perfume surrounded her.

"Look who's all high and mighty in a fancy uniform," she said, glaring at me through her round, tortoise-shell glasses. "Talk about a pig in a poke bonnet."

"Hi, Miss Brumutt," I said. "Would you like some water?"

"Of course I would, if it's fit to drink."

"I'm sure it is."

"The water supply was replenished in Winnipeg," said Louis, who was seating folks across the aisle. "It's the same water you drink from the city tap."

"I suppose it'll be okay," Miss Brumutt said. Have you washed your hands, Bobby Bates?"

"Yes, Ma'am." I suppressed the urge to scowl at her use of the diminutive, *Bobby*. She'd done that with all my classmates, a way to keep us in our place.

I reached for the menu on the far side of the table. "Careful of my new hat, Bobby," she snapped, shaking her head and clucking her tongue.

"You write your choice on this slip of paper," I said.

"I have to write my own dinner order?"

"That's the way it's done on the train," I said.

"I thought I was taking the luxury route to visit my sister in Saskatoon," she barked, snatching the pencil out of my hand. "Is this some third world train?"

"You'll find a similar system on all Class 1 railways," Louis said. "Bob, start picking up orders. I can assist the lady."

"I am perfectly capable of writing my own." Miss Brumutt waved Louis away.

I returned the water pitcher to the galley and began picking up orders. When I reached Miss Brumutt's table she sported the same triumphant expression she wore when handing back French tests—tests that I often failed or barely squeaked through because the atmosphere in her class made me too uptight to absorb anything.

I glanced at her order. *Soupe au poulet, Pommes de terre frites, Saumon…* "Miss Brumutt, you've written this in French." I tried to hand it back to her.

She waved my hand away. "Bobby Bates, I'm sure you'll have no problem interpreting my schoolteacher handwriting."

"The steward is bilingual, but I'm not sure about the kitchen staff. Could you please rewrite—"

"Certainly not. I hope you absorbed enough from my classes to interpret a simple menu in French."

Knowing it was useless to argue with Glad Ass Mutt, I carried the orders to the galley. I handed them to the chef, then picked up a silver tray loaded with half a dozen bowls containing soup or salad. Balancing the tray on one hand, I staggered to the first table, almost losing my balance as we rose and fell over a grade crossing. I knew the F9 diesels at the head end had a top speed of 89 mph, and glancing out the window at the blur of roadbed and prairie dust being kicked up, it looked like Stampede Mike was giving them free rein.

I pressed my thigh firmly against the table and began serving the soups and salads, then on to the next table. I lurched back to the galley for another tray, almost knocking over one of the other waiters.

Louis steadied me with a hand on my back. "Remember what I said, Bob. Just relax—move *with* the train."

Miss Brumutt wasn't so kind. "Bobby, you're staggering around *comme un singe ivre*, like a drunken monkey," she said when I reached her table with my loaded tray. "Are you liquored up?"

"It's my first day on the job," I said as I passed salads to the family seated at her table.

They nodded understandingly, the woman saying, "I'm sure you'll get the hang of it."

"If you'd had him as a student in your French class you wouldn't be so sure of that," Miss Brumutt said, chortling in her diabolical facsimile of a laugh.

"Here's your soupe au poulet, Miss Brumutt. I hope you'll enjoy it," I said, suppressing the temptation to dump it into her lap. I didn't want my first day to be my last.

She picked up her spoon and dipped it gingerly into the soup. It looked as if she suspected a school of hungry piranhas might be lurking beneath its surface. I turned to head back to the galley, but not soon enough.

"Bobby, this soup tastes like dishwater. It's insipid, bland." She pointed to the offending bowl. "It needs a healthy shake of salt, a wee bit of pepper."

"There's salt and pepper on the table," I said, pointing to the shakers.

"But if I season it myself, the chef won't know his recipe is a failure, will he?"

"No, I guess not, Miss Brumutt." I picked up her soup and carried it back to the galley. The chef was not amused, but sprinkled half a teaspoon of salt into the bowl and a hearty grind of pepper, gave it a stir, and set it on my tray. It was a slow trip to the far table as I weaved my way past the other waiters. The old mutt would probably complain the soup was tepid by the time I got it back to her.

The next moments remain a slow-motion horror movie in my mind. There was a rush of wind and an awful racket of steel wheels on steel rails as someone breached the door between the dome and dining car. At the same moment the train passed over a road crossing, causing Louis, who was serving the table on the other side of the aisle, to rock back on his heels. His elbow bumped the silver tray holding Miss Brumutt's freshly-seasoned soup. I raised my arm, hoping to move the tray out of his way. In doing so, the edge nabbed the feathers on Miss Brumutt's hat. I tried to steady the tray but it tilted, sending the bowl of soup skidding to the edge where it tipped, dumping its contents into the brim of Miss Brumutt's pheasant-adorned chapeau.

If she had remained seated, like I warned her to, she'd have left the soup to slosh around her hat brim like water in a castle's moat. Instead, she leapt to her feet. The brim angled forward, spilling soup over the tablecloth, onto the floor, and finally dropping oily globs of chicken parts and noodles onto her white blouse.

"Idiot! You incompetent idiot! You stupid, stupid—"

"It was *my* fault," Louis said, handing me his tray while elbowing me out of the way. He snatched a napkin from one of the other diners and began pawing at Miss Brumutt's shoulders and chest.

"Leave it. Leave it alone." Miss Brumutt swatted Louis' hands. "You're rubbing the stain in."

"Get the mop and some towels," Louis said.

I staggered away to the locker at the far end of the car where the cleaning supplies were kept. When I got back, both Louis and Miss Brumutt had disappeared. I apologized to the family, who despite the mess, were taking it pretty well. In fact, they were struggling to suppress their laughter. I had the slop cleaned up by the time Louis got back.

"I'm sorry about that," I said.

"It wasn't your fault, Bob."

"Will she sue me?"

"She's ordering the conductor to toss you off the train, but he'll write her a chit for a new blouse and hat, and probably refund her ticket too. I'll take a tray to her roomette in a few minutes. You get on with serving the main course."

He put a hand on my shoulder. "Didn't I say it'd be a sloppy trip?"

Stone Walls
Robert Ramsay

I'm standing on the ladder, a brush in one hand, a bucket of red paint in the other. The prairie sun is beating down, but I can't complain. If I'd kept my mouth shut at breakfast, I might be playing in my shade-dappled tree house across the road in the big bush.

"Dad, why did Great-Grandfather paint those red lines on the front wall of the stone house?" I had asked while spreading Mom's homemade strawberry jam on my second slice of toast.

"Shush, Kyle. I'm listening to the weather," Dad said, turning up the volume on the radio. "I need to know if it's safe to cut the alfalfa. It'll need four drying days after I bring it down."

By the time Dad switched off the radio, I'd forgotten my question about the red lines, but he hadn't. "It was your Scottish great-grandmother's idea to paint those lines over the mortar and stones. She wanted the house to look like it was built of dressed stone."

"Dressed stone?"

"They're stones that have been squared off like bricks. Perhaps in Scotland a field stone cottage like this house was considered lower class."

"The lines are fading," I said. "You can't see them from the road."

"Now, there's a job for you," Dad had said. "After you've fed and watered the calves you can touch up those lines. There's a can of oxblood paint left over from when we painted the barn."

It's tedious work for a nine-year-old boy. First, I sweep the walls to remove the spider webs and bits of crumbling mortar from between the stones. Then, starting at the top, I begin painting over the lines, back and forth, up and down. When I've finished the first part, top to bottom, I run onto the lawn and turn to survey my work. From a distance it looks as though the wall is built of squared-off stones, big enough to keep out the wildest weather.

I move the ladder over and begin at the top once again. I've been working for an hour when Grandma, who lives in a white frame cottage across the lane, comes to take a look. "You must be working up a powerful thirst in this heat," she says, handing me a tall tumbler of ice-cold lemonade. I thank her and snug the cool wetness against my paint-spattered cheek, before gulping down the lemonade.

"Did you grow up in this house?" I ask, as she bends over the flowerbed to make sure I haven't trampled the red petunias which are surrounded by whispers of white baby's breath.

"My sisters and I shared the big bedroom over the kitchen," she says.

"Did you ever bang your head on the ceiling?"

"I did. Those sloping ceilings were responsible for many an Ouch!"

"Mom wants Dad to build a new house," I say, handing the empty tumbler back to Grandma.

"Ach, it's a case of your mother's been sketching plans for a new house since the day she married your father." Grandma turns to go. "But I doubt she'll ever budge your father. He was born in the front bedroom upstairs, same as me and my sisters."

I resume my painting. In my head, I replay the argument Mom and Dad had that morning, an argument they've been having for weeks.

"Alastair, aren't you ashamed to see me wheeling this old ringer machine into the kitchen every time I wash clothes?"

"What's wrong with it, Phyllis? Is it broken?"

"You know what I mean. Your sister, Alice, has a new automatic washer. All she has to do is throw the clothes in and push a button."

"If it's an automatic washer you want, I'll get you one."

"And where would you put it inside this crumbling pile of stones?"

"I could build a lean-to onto the summer kitchen."

"I don't want a lean-to. I want a proper bungalow with three bedrooms like Harold built for Alice."

"You've got five bedrooms upstairs," Dad said, taking his cap and gloves from the shelf by the back door. "I can run the plumbing up to one of the spare rooms if you want an automatic washer."

I can't blame Mom for wanting a new washing machine. It's hard work filling the tub with water and running the clothes through the wringer. But it's not just the washing machine. She wants a new kitchen, one like Auntie Alice's, with a built-in oven and a refrigerator that makes ice on hot summer days like today. She wants a new bathroom too, one with a proper shower stall and twin sinks like Auntie Alice's.

It takes all morning and most of the afternoon to paint the lines on the front of the house. When I'm finished and have put the ladder and paint away, I jump onto my bike and pedal to the end of the lane, startling the grasshoppers who rise from the gravel, their wings clicking against each other. I ride slowly past our yard, admiring how the lines make it look like the house is built of huge blocks of dressed stone.

After supper, Dad follows me out the lane. He points west to where the sun is hidden behind a wall of dark thunderheads. "There was nothing about rain in the forecast," he says, "so I hope those clouds are empties."

When we reach the road, we turn, and as if on cue, the sun peeks through the clouds, bathing the stone house in the evening light. The pale pinks, dusty blues, and greys of the fieldstones glow with a touch of gold, freshly framed by the brick-like lines in oxblood red.

"You've done a real good job, Kyle," Dad says. "Your Great-Grandmother would be pleased if she could see this. I hadn't realized how much those lines had faded."

He gives me a hug, then straightens up and surveys the rest of our buildings. There's the big red barn, the Holsteins gathered around the smudge Dad lit to keep the mosquitoes and flies off their backs. The chicken house squats beside it, the south wall a row of windows so the sun can keep our Rhode Island Red layers warm and happy. There's a tool shed, and then the white picket fence surrounding Grandma's cottage.

"That chicken house is looking bedraggled," Dad says. "If I buy another can of oxblood paint, can you give it a touch-up?"

Back in the stone house, Dad settles himself in his armchair to read *The Country Guide*. I head upstairs, loving the feel of the smooth banister carved by Great-Grandfather. I sometimes go into the tool shed and look through his tool chest, admiring the chisels and planes he used to decorate the staircase with Scotch thistles painted in soft shades of mauve and green.

Upstairs, I grab *The Adventures of Sammy Jay* off my bedside table. I yank the patchwork quilt off my bed and heave it onto the deep windowsill. I make a nest for myself, then clamber up, and drawing my knees up to my chin, sit in my secret hideaway in the dormer. Gentle puffs of air flutter through the screen. There's the acrid smell of the smudge in the barnyard, then the scent of red and yellow roses blooming in the cottage muddle in front of Grandma's house, then the medicine-like odour of pine pitch as the evening breeze changes direction once again.

I'm distracted from Sammy Jay's adventures by robins trolling for worms on the lawn under the old oak tree. I watch them cock their heads from side to side. Are they able to hear the worms, I wonder? Do earthworms make a rustling sound while gliding through the soil, same as the garter snakes I find in the long grass behind the house?

Suddenly, in a fluster of feathers, the robins skedaddle. I watch to see what has startled them. A moment later Solomon Grundy, our handsome rooster, strides onto the lawn, the setting sun flashing rainbows from his plumage as he inspects his kingdom before taking to his roost for the night.

Looking beyond the fence and the road, I see the big bush. Deer, foxes and wolves make it their home. As the sun blobs on the horizon, the bush is in shadow, the tallest trees sending monstrous arms and fingers creeping across the lawn. I listen for the wolves, but they aren't howling yet. Perhaps it's too early—they like to wait for dark nights with a full moon—or perhaps they've noticed the black clouds and are taking cover in their dens.

Suddenly there's a flash of light, followed by a distant crack of thunder. I hear Dad's footsteps on the stairway. "Are you up here, Kyle?"

"I'm in my room."

Dad looks in, sees me sitting on the dormer's sill. "Better close that window. Come into the sun porch with me. We'll watch the storm from up here."

The sun porch, built over the front entranceway that no one ever uses, has windows on three sides. As the wind picks up, and the evergreens lining the lane sway back and forth, I feel like I'm the captain of a ship, steering a course through the angry waves.

Flashes of lightning bring the boiling clouds into sharp focus and every few seconds a fork of electricity plunges from the sky. Dad and I watch as one strikes the barn, sizzling down the cable connecting the lightning rod to the ground. Another hits the old oak tree near where the robins were feeding on the lawn, another the lightning rod on Grandma's cottage. I see her lights blink out, then wink back on. There's a moment of silence before a final flaming dagger scores a direct hit on the stone house. I let out a yell and cling to Dad's arm as the charge zaps down the cable siding the porch, the instant thunder shaking the whole house. A sharp odour seeps through the cracks around the window.

"What's that smell, Dad?"

"That's the lightning ripping the air apart. You're smelling ozone."

And then, just as suddenly as it came, the storm is gone, marching east to display its fury to the neighbours.

Mom comes up the stairs. "Quite a storm, eh?" She's carrying a pen and paper.

"But only a few drops of rain," Dad says. "Should be a good drying day for the alfalfa tomorrow."

"Why didn't you watch the storm with us?" I ask.

"I've been sketching." Mom sits beside Dad. She hands him the paper. "Take a look at this, Alastair. Tell me what you think."

I perch on the arm of the loveseat and lean on Dad's shoulder to watch as Mom guides us through the rooms: a big kitchen with a built-in oven and double sink, a laundry room, a proper bathroom, a family room with a stone fireplace.

"Where are the bedrooms?" I ask.

"I guess your father is right. We have enough bedrooms," Mom says. "You see, Alastair, you could build on at the back of this house—make a door where the kitchen window is."

"This morning you said you didn't want a lean-to."

"I don't, but we could build so the addition blends in with the walls and roof of this house. What do you think?"

Dad takes the sketch, turns it this way and that, then looks at me. His lips are a tight line. Then he opens and smacks them together the way he does when he knows he's beat. "All right, Phyllis. We'll go to the lumberyard tomorrow. We'll estimate the cost."

Mom hugs Dad and pulls him up by the hand. They do a little dance around the sun porch.

I scurry to my room, shed my clothes, pull on my pajamas, then yank the quilt off the windowsill and toss it over my bed. I crawl under the covers and close my eyes.

I'm awakened sometime later by a blood-thirsty screech. I run to the window. There's another screech and then the owl that lives in the dead cottonwood behind the house, swoops past, it's wing tip brushing the glass. I crawl back into bed and snuggle deep under the covers.

I'm glad to be safe inside the thick walls of the stone house.

Tall Tails
Robert Ramsay

Heat and humidity make me ill. They slow me down physically and mentally. In fact, it was the hot, humid summers of Southern Ontario that inspired me to flee to the west coast when I retired. The eastern winters I could tolerate, even enjoy. There was nothing as exciting as a tramp along traffic-bereft streets during a February blizzard, my parka-clad head bowed against the howling winds and driving snows. But the heat's a killer, driving all sane thought out of my mind, so you'll understand why the summer of 2018 in White Rock was particularly difficult for me.

The extreme heat and the smoke from the devastating forest fires forced me to curtail my usual activities. I had to give up the habit of beginning the day with a stroll down to the pier followed by a brisk hike up Oxford Street. It was too uncomfortable even to sit on a log at East Beach, watching the dogs hightail it after sticks and balls. For the most part, I hunkered down indoors, especially after Fiona fled to the cottage in Sechelt with our daughter and two grandkids.

   For three weeks I was left at home to water the vegetable garden and keep Mr. Queue company. He had no more desire to venture outdoors than did I, preferring to spend his days curled up on the cold hearthstone. No doubt the mice and shrews he liked to proudly drop at my feet enjoyed the temporary reprieve.

   I took cold showers and caught up on my reading. I started with *On the Devil's Tail: in Combat with the Waffen-SS*. It recounts the war experiences of a young Italian man in Europe and later, Indo-China. It was pretty heavy going, though, so when I tired of the killing fields I dipped into *Under the Dragon's Tail*, a Murdoch Mystery. It's one of Fiona's books, but when the wife's away the cat will play, right? Not that I'd tell anyone, especially the grandkids. They've reached the teen years so they'd think their granddad odd if they caught me reading such lite fare.

   When I wanted a break from watering the garden and reading, I entertained myself by watching Mr. Queue play with his tail. As he pounced and pawed in a constant whirl of catch-me-if-you-can, I wondered why humans didn't have tails. If we had tails—not little bunny tails, but long tails like those of cougars, monkeys and raccoons—we'd have no need of cell phones. In quiet moments, we could entertain ourselves like Mr. Queue does, by chasing our tails instead of staring at a hand-held device.

   Of course, our first challenge would be to work out the details. We'd have to decide whether the tail was an erotic part of the body. Some august gathering of spiritually-minded persons would be convened to consider the matter. It would likely take them several months to determine the true meaning of biblical passages like this one from Job: *He moveth his tail like a cedar: the sinews of his stones are wrapped together.*

And what about this one from The Revelation? *For their power is in their mouth, and in their tails: for their tails were like unto serpents, and had heads, and with them they do hurt.* Such a clear warning would require several months of reverent review.

If the theologians pronounced the tail responsible for inciting sexual feelings, the unmentionable member would have to be concealed in public. How would we do this?

Would we simply poke our tail down one of our pant legs, or would we hire tailors to sew tailpipes onto our pants to enclose the tail? And would this extra piece of clothing be made of the same fabric as the pant legs, or would it have its own character, black leather studded with rivets perhaps, like a rear-ended codpiece? Perhaps they would come in many different colours and materials and could be changed every day to match our shoes, scarves or ties.

Would sexual desirability be determined by the size of our tails? If so, our email accounts would be flooded with messages promising to alter their size. Some physicians would specialize in tail-reduction surgery for those who were too heavily endowed. For those with disappointingly meager members, manufacturers would offer falsies that would make their tails look quite robust inside their decorative sheaths.

And what about those who still wanted to wear dresses, skirts and kilts? Would they require a train-like appendage, perhaps fashioned from satin and decorated with sequins? Or would they let their tails hang down inside their skirts, the more adventuresome ones permitting just the tip to show below the hem?

Would television preachers decry short skirts and revealed tailage as a sign of the end of the world? When walking behind women on the street, would polite men refuse to lower their eyes, fearing they might be accused of tailgating?

On the other hand, if the tail was categorized as an appendage without any sexual allure, it could be left to swing freely. A suitable opening would be provided in clothing to allow the tail to swing about while one walked. Ladies might decorate their tails with ribbons and bows while men might shave theirs, perhaps creating unique and attractive designs with their razors. Of course, in the colder climates woolen tailings would be worn. Grandmothers skilled with knitting needles would have another outlet for their creativity. During holiday seasons we might decorate our tails with coloured balls, tinkling bells and sparkling taillights.

Retailers would need to modify their furniture. Chairs might be provided with tail pipes in the back centre of the seat, into which one would carefully insert one's tail as one settled down. Similar pipes would be required in cars, on trains, buses and airplanes. Those with extra long tails would request seats in the tail section of the aircraft where the pipes could be extended without compromising the comfort of other travelers.

When walking down the narrow aisles on a transit bus or in an aircraft one would have to be careful. It would be poor manners to swish one's tail so as to knock the drink out of some fellow passenger's hand, or worse yet, whip one's tail right into the mouth of someone who was yawning.

Boy, it's hot. I better go water the garden again.

"You coming out for a bit, Mr. Queue? You can tell me whether you think it would be a good idea for us humans to have tails. I'm sure the researchers who are genetically modifying our food could modify our bodies to give us tails as handsome as yours.

"Just think of all the new services and consumer products that would be needed. The increased economic activity might prevent the global economy from spiraling into a deadly tailspin.

"Come along, Mr. Queue. Let's hightail it out to the garden before it gets any hotter."

The Problem of Self-Stimulation
Robert Ramsay

Self-stimulation*: stimulation of oneself as a result of one's own activity or behavior (electrical self–stimulation of the brain in rats)*
Merriam-Webster online medical dictionary.

When self-stimulation became rampant in the first decade of the twenty-first century, I expected that governments would pass regulatory laws. I assumed that others were as sickened by the abusive practice as I was, and that lawmakers at local, provincial and federal levels would take swift action.

I thought municipal councilors would designate certain areas as free from this societal curse, such as they have done with smoking—no self-stimulation within ten metres of a building's entrance, no self-stimulation in public parks or restaurants.

I was confident that legislators would see the financial and human toll self-stimulation exacts via road accidents and lost productivity in the workplace. I expected them to pass stringent laws against the practice. At the very least, I expected the feds would ban self-stimulation in airports, except in designated rooms outfitted with frosted glass to prevent children getting the wrong impression about what constitutes healthy social intercourse.

My expectations have not been realized, and so, in this election year, I raise the issue for public debate. I suppose the Conservatives, no longer progressive, will insist that government has no right binding citizens' hands. The New Democratic Party will promise a National Self-Stimulation Program, which will net us a ministry of bureaucrats who do nothing but play with their own taxpayer-funded devices. The Liberals, fresh from legalizing marijuana, will be too busy smoking pot to recognize there's a problem. The Greens will turn a blind eye to self-stimulation so long as it doesn't involve burning fossil fuels. Meanwhile the abusive practice will continue, draining this nation of its vital juices.

Some years back, I was in the City of Coquitlam, examining progress on the Evergreen rapid transit line. My visit coincided with the end of the school day. The sidewalks were awash with fine looking youth, their faces flushed with the thrill of learning. They had to pass beneath the transit gangways where tool-belt wearing construction workers were standing. Even though modern society frowns upon such lewd behaviour, I expected to hear one or two wolf whistles. There was not a single peep. The hard-hatted construction workers and students alike were bent over their instruments, their fingers whirring lustfully.

Anthology

On the way home I had to drive through the construction zone. Two flag ladies were directing traffic. Both had their SLOW/STOP signs tucked beneath their arms, while they bent over their gadgets, fingers flying as though performing a typing speed test. Apparently motorists' lives were of no value to these ladies.

In times past I could board a transit bus expecting to meet someone of interest. The person sitting or standing beside me would smile, say a few words, and the trip would pass pleasantly as we commented on the world's wild weather, our rebellious teenagers, or our latest skirmish with the health system. No longer! Now when I board the bus, the majority of riders are already bent over their tools. If not, two seconds after I sit down, my seatmate will whip his device out and begin self-manipulation.

Being a person of Christian faith, I am ashamed to admit that this wicked practice has penetrated the nation's churches. Congregants, claiming to be reading their Bibles or memorizing hymn lyrics, are instead pounding their wee things. They think the priest in the pulpit cannot see how addicted they are to this pernicious habit, but their bowed heads and bobbling fingers give them away.

The most recent incident, that impels me to spend a sunny afternoon indoors writing this essay, occurred along White Rock's seaside promenade. I was strolling along, enjoying the view of sailboats tacking across the bay. Gulls were trolling the sea for scraps, robins were hopping across the grass, and a posse of crows was fighting over an errant fish and chip box. It was one of those moments when all seemed right in the world.

Then, coming towards me, I saw a young lady pushing a stroller. Her toddler, a boy if his blue jump suit was an indication of gender, was goo-gooing and gaa-gaaing in celebration of the delightful day. Like most two-year-olds he had a few questions to pose about his environment.

"Mommy? Bird? Bird?" he chirped, pointing at the robin.

"Mommy? Daddy? Daddy?" He was pointing at me.

I expected Mommy to follow the trajectory of her wee son's finger and correct his mistaken impression that I was his daddy, but she did no such thing. She didn't care that her child was going to grow up thinking that every strange man was his daddy.

Why didn't she care? You guessed it. She was bent over her tool, her fingers, like the wings of a hummingbird, invisible. I wouldn't be surprised if at the moment the child was conceived both she and the child's daddy were quite unaware of their actions because both were madly playing with their own personal devices.

Is this what we want for our children and grandchildren? Do we want them to be so devoted to their hand-held idols that they are unaware of real life happening around them? Do we want them to settle for a pseudo brand of social intercourse that burdens them with a core loneliness that no cyber friends can assuage? Should we not, before it is too late, warn them of the lonely consequences of self-stimulation?

Some may protest that our politicians have addressed this issue by outlawing auto stimulation in moving vehicles, but I say this is too little, too late. A significant amount of life is lived outside of moving vehicles. Consider for a moment the world in which we would live if these devices had been in use during our nation-building days. Would the Fathers of Confederation have succeeded in their deliberations if they had spent the whole week posing for selfies in front of Charlottetown's Government House? Would the Canadian Pacific Railway have been built if our Chinese brothers had stood about worshiping their tools instead of putting pick and shovel to earth? What if Laura Secord had dawdled to diddle with her gizmo instead of hiking twenty miles to report American plans to the British? Today we would not be enjoying her Fruit Flavoured Jellied Candy or her Truffles Sprinkled with Cocoa Powder.

During this election year I challenge all would-be politicians to grab hold of this issue with both hands. I urge them to propose legislation that will pull the plug on this plague of self-stimulation. May they find the courage to direct Canadians back to the good old days when social intercourse was carried out face to face.

Writings from The Oval Table

Anthology

A Group Writing Exercise

The Mysterious Affair at The Corner Café

(The following story was written as a group exercise. Kathy began the story and each member of the Oval Table continued with the next section.)

Accidents happen. Just yesterday while I was having lunch at the café on the corner, the waitress turned quickly and ran into a customer who was getting out of his chair. Her tray of drinks teetered and one glass of wine crashed to the floor. Wine spattered everywhere and pieces of glass scattered. Was the waitress careless? If she had been more careful, would the accident not have happened? What about the customer, should he have been more careful? These are the questions that haunt me.

(Continued by Doreen)

I was supposed to be working at home today. Finding it difficult to concentrate, I decided to take a walk and drop into The Corner Café. Mary, the waitress who had been involved in the small accident yesterday, was there but not working. She was sitting at a small corner table. I could see she'd been crying. I asked if I could join her. She silently motioned for me to sit.

"I think they are going to fire me," she volunteered. "That man has been harassing me for months, working at getting me into trouble. Yesterday, as I passed his table, he touched my calf with something. Then, when I turned round with the full tray, he got up and purposely bumped into me. He's in the back speaking with the owners now. Says he's injured his neck and shoulder and is going to sue. I don't know what to do."

I was shocked into silence. I have been coming here once a week for two years. Mary is always both friendly and efficient. When I found my voice, I said, "Mary I believe you. What we need is a plan to expose him or at least make sure you keep your job."

(Continued by David)

"I wouldn't know where to begin," said Mary. "It seems almost hopeless."

Looking deep into Mary's eyes, I said, "Perhaps it doesn't look good, but remember, every cloud has a silver lining. Well, almost always."

"What should I do?"

"I suggest you catch the boss when he has a free moment. Then calmly explain your side of the story"

"I'll do that as soon as I can. Actually, I do know the boss appreciates my hard work."

"See Mary, there you go. Things are looking up."

"But what about this fellow who has been bullying me? You know, I don't even know his name. How should I deal with him?"

"Mary, I'm sure the boss will talk to him."

"But, what if he won't?"

"You have two brothers, don't you Mary?"

"Actually, I have three—three older brothers."

"Well, there you have it. I'm sure they can use their powers of persuasion."

(Continued by Karen)

"You mean Lorenzo, Mosè and Guido?"

"You have a brother named Guido?"

"Yes, I do. Oh, that's not the name we called him when he was growing up but when he lost his curls and became follicly challenged, seemingly over night, he dropped his childhood moniker and insisted we call him by his official name."

Our conversation was interrupted by shouts from the back room. "I'll give you just one week to come up with a reasonable offer," the bully threatened. "I'll be back next Tuesday at noon. If you don't have the cash, I'll call my lawyer!"

Mary shook as the man stormed passed her. Once she caught her breath she continued, "Oddly, around the time he lost his hair, Guido discovered the Society of Friends, converted, then persuaded his brothers to join him. Who knew my rabble-rousing brothers would become peace-loving Quakers?!"

"You're kidding. Did they change their work too?"

"No, they still run their gym, *The Toned Brothers*, and do personal training on the side. Despite their new religious stance, they continue with their music—a string trio playing at local events. I swear Larry can make that cello sing. No imagination. They still call their band *The Toned Brothers*."

A dreamy look filled Mary's eyes as she continued, "They are absolutely stunning in their fedoras and pin-striped suits." With a chuckle she added, "When they enter the room with their instrument cases, women swoon and I've watched blood drain from grown men's faces."

I said nothing, just waited for the ball to drop. Finally Mary gasped, "You've given me a great idea! I'm going to call Moe right now and arrange for my brothers to drop by on the way to their gig next Tuesday afternoon."

(Continued by Robert)

All week I puzzled over what I'd witnessed in The Corner Café on that afternoon. Something wasn't quite right but I couldn't figure out just what it was—maybe the way Mary's lower lip quivered when she was telling me her story, or maybe the way she turned off her tears when waxing eloquent about her brothers' fedoras and suits.

Since she hadn't said just when her brothers would be dropping by, I made sure I was at my usual table by a quarter to twelve on Tuesday. I knew that was early for anyone to be going to a gig, but I didn't want to miss the showdown, no matter what time it started.

While waiting for Mary and her brothers to arrive I

ordered a coffee and a donut, then pulled out my smart phone and called everyone I knew. When I ran out of friends, I googled *The Toned Brothers*. Wikipedia told essentially the same story Mary had told me the previous week. It added that their last name was Fortissimo. Another interesting fact was that Mary, their only sister, had, during the brothers' gang period, married rival gang member Tony Pianissimo.

This struck a fishy-sounding note for me. Hadn't I read something about Tony in *The Daily* just the previous week, something about him being down on his luck, his used musical instrument business being seized by the city, being put on the auction block for payment of back taxes?

And hadn't that been Tony I had seen and heard in the kitchen, threatening The Corner Café's owner to pay up or else? At the time I thought he looked familiar, but couldn't remember that I'd just seen his picture in the paper. That was what had been bothering me all week.

Obviously I had been duped by Mary's tearful tale. She and Tony must have planned the whole lawsuit deal. If they had their way they would bring The Corner Café to its knees so they could solve their own financial worries. But what role did *The Toned Brothers* have in all this? Why did Mary want them to show up? Were they planning to form a quartet with Tony the moment he'd squeezed cash out of The Corner Café's rightful owner? Were they planning to use the cash to buy The Corner Café, then turn it into Tony's Tuneful Tymes, a hangout for classical musicians?

Anthology

POETRY

The Things I Carry
A prose poem by Karen Shaw

The things I carry are in an imaginary suitcase
filled with my favourite intangible items.
Only I know where it is.
Only I can access it.
This light-weight luggage is always available,
a toolbox at my fingertips.
My travel bag's only limitations,
the boundaries of my creativity.

During difficult medical procedures,
I summon my favourite songs.
When bored,
plan the next family gathering.
If caught in traffic,
dream of a better scenario.
My travel bag's only limitations,
the boundaries of my creativity.

Small things conjure up memories from childhood.
When life closes in and depression strikes,
I recall a friend's voice with encouraging words.
I re-use my preferred dreams
or change their endings on a whim.
My travel bag's only limitations,
the boundaries of my creativity.

Exhausted,
at the end of a frenetic day,
I book a ticket to My Island.
There, as other residents gather berries
on the opposite side of that tropical paradise,
I curl up in my hammock on the beach.
the warm breezes rock my swaying cot,

tease my hair while gentle waves lap at the shore.
The rhythms melt away my tension.
I awaken to another dawn
to gather, sort and repack my suitcase
with more of my favourite things.
The boundaries of my creativity
my only limitations.

The Eternal Dance
Doreen Tadros

Fog shrouds the sea in eerie gloom
Waves drum out a haunting tune
The wind, excited, roils the ocean
To churning pot of witch's potion
A symphony rising to the sky
As waves crash, spraying mist on high

The waves swirl now in manic dance
As wanton waifs, they tempt and prance
The rocks, entranced, allow embrace
Joining forces, face to face
Never more will they be free
Caught in lock step with the sea
Doomed to dance eternally

Haiku
by Karen Shaw

his young eyes, so proud
as he presents his treasure—
dandelion bouquet

    sizzling sun, cool breeze
    sand ripples beneath my feet
    icy waves on toes

        take my breath away
        old, abandoned apple tree
        fruit still crisp and sweet

            delicate snowdrops
            from whence comes your energy
            to dispel the snow?

Child of War
Doreen Tadros

I live the horrors of warfare,
Lost my family to a bomb.
I'm just a small child crying,
Longing for Mother's hug and kiss.

For years I've fended for myself
Among ruins pock-marked by war;
Stealing food from trucks and stores,
Dirty streets, garbage cans, the dump.

All this time I've carried with me
My little sister's broken doll,
Witness to a life cut short.
I see her before me, smiling.

I am a child of warfare
Caught in a grown-ups' fight,
Struggling for survival
Amid guns, violence, death.

I spend each day in hiding
Or dodging bullets, men and tanks.
A child, frightened and alone
Feeling loss, pain, despair.

I cry myself to sleep each night
Huddling in a burnt-out car--
A fitful sleep with nightmares;
Children's screams, bodies, bombs.

That this war will soon be over
Is my hope and dream each day.
But I know I'll never feel again
The warmth of Mother's hug and kiss.

September
Doreen Tadros

Light your fire, sip your wine
September's here, heralding change
Cooler days, chilly nights
Summer's dying

Camping's over for another year
With campfires and marshmallows
And lazy days stretching into night
Summer, won't you stay?

The days are getting shorter
Sometimes Winter shows his face
Beat him back, September
There's still time to love and laze

Leaves turn orange, red and gold
The colours of September
Soon October will dance with you
Dressed in solemn brown

October, don't let Winter in
Push him far away
Soon enough he'll hold us
Indoors by warm firesides

Anthology

'Til then we have September
With lingering sun and autumn flowers
Long walks and barbecues
September, please stay a while

Seasons of Love
Doreen Tadros

As the wind is free, be free
Blow gently when you pass my way
Caress me with your breath
I shall await the gentle breezes of your love

Like the snow, fall gently on me
Cover me with the soft protective
Blanket of your love
That I'll not feel the cold nor fear its pain

As the rain, come to me
Wash my body with your tears
And, as a summer shower
Refresh me and give me life

As the sun, shine on me
Let me bask in your tender warmth
Enfold me in your arms
Let me feel the heat and passion of your love

Look at me, I am the moon
Reflecting back to you
The beauty of your love
And bathing you in the soft light of mine

Two Limericks by Doreen Tadros
(Written for the White Rock Irish Festival)

A sweet Irish lassie came here
To play on our beach and drink beer
"Mayor Baldwin", she said
"I sure hurt my head
When I fell from that rock near your pier."

A young Irish lass with red hair
Sat on White Rock Pier in fresh air
When painted all green
She felt like a queen
But, apart from the paint, was quite bare.

The Roses
Doreen Tadros

They brought roses
In a vase
Placed them thoughtfully
On the windowsill
"Thank you," I whispered
Beautiful, I thought
Red, silken, perfect
Like my youth
Then I slept

For weeks I watched those roses
Colour faded, petals thinned
They didn't die
Just dried up
That's me, I thought
Not dead, just dried up
Paler, fading, sear
No longer vibrant
Then I slept

The secret of life in those roses
Sliding down toward death
Do we dry up and wither away?
Immobile now, yet unafraid
I've had my day
Many adventures, much work
Strong, vital, alive
Youthful memories
Then I slept

Now I lie here
Knowing when the water is gone
When it's all dried up
I'll meet my maker
Well, I've loved, been loved
Laughed, cried, lived
Kissed my children
Loved them above everything
Now they visit
With roses
In a vase
Soon I'll sleep

Butterflies
Doreen Tadros

The butterfly knew life before
Dimly in her memory
Her feet firmly on the ground
Crawling

Awakening now, a delicate beauty
Feelings of lightness
Yes, wings, a new freedom
Flying

But the wings, how fragile they are
How quickly damaged
No longer strong enough to fly
Dying

Like the butterfly, I too remember
A past life on the ground
Weary paths my feet have trod
Walking

Your love gave me wings like her
Wings fine as gossamer
With you I learned to fly
Flying

Anthology

You had no faith to fly with me
Shredded now, torn and bruised
Crushed by a careless hand
Crying
Dying

A Tough Row to Hoe
Robert Ramsay

The cliché is said to be a horrid thing,
Yet some have quite a pleasant ring.
Why then, do editors go ape
And get themselves bent out of shape
When I submit my literary bling?

    Why do they call me on the carpet,
    Work themselves into such a sweat?
    Why call me an ignorant buffoon,
    Urging me to change my tune?
    Clichés are my best asset.

Editors leave me at wits' end;
Their rejections send me 'round the bend.
They label me a lazy lout,
My poems, a complete washout.
Can't they appreciate my scholarly blend?

    They brand my lines a nasty wreck,
    Refuse to write a big, fat cheque;
    Give me not a ghost of a chance
    To join the writer's dance—
    They'd like to wring my neck.

Editors call my prose an ugly toad,
Way beyond the mother lode.
They label me a terrible bore,
Shove me right out the door,
Order me to choose another mode.

    Yet, faithful readers abound.
    Most sit spellbound.
    They never bust a gut,
    Or kick me in the butt.
    They find my lines quite sound.

My prose is cute as a bug's ear,
The sort folks like to hear.
It's cut and dried,
Loved worldwide,
Better than Shakespeare.

    My words are dressed to kill,
    Designed to give quite a thrill.
    I'm sure you are agreeing
    With every fibre of your being
    As you admire my writing skill.

Editors, lay aside your angry look
And let me off the hook.
I don't need a shrink,
For quick as a wink
I'm about to write another book.

Anthology

Just a Moment in Time
Doreen Tadros

As I walk along the water's edge,
I turn to see my footsteps in the sand.
Looking out over the vastness of the ocean
I start to dream.

Is this the first time I've walked this earth?
Was I among the very first fish to step out of the sea,
Making the very first footprints
In the sand?

Did I follow in Christ's footsteps
Beside the sea of Galilee,
Listening to his message of love?
Was I there?

Is it possible that I stepped onto the bus
And sat in the back watching
As Rosa Parks bravely walked toward the front?
Did I cower in fear?

Maybe I marched the city streets
With Martin Luther King as he led his people
Toward his dream of freedom
Was it my dream too?

Anthology

I stop my reverie and turn again to see the flat sand
Where my footprints showed just moments ago
Like the fleeting moments of our lives
Just a moment in time.

If you enjoyed this book we'd appreciate it if you would write an online review.

Made in the USA
Middletown, DE
13 March 2019